TRADE AND INVESTMENT
IN THE MIDDLE EAST

Rodney Wilson

First published 1977 by
THE MACMILLAN PRESS LTD
London and Basingstoke
Associated companies in Delhi
Dublin Hong Kong Johannesburg Lagos
Melbourne New York Singapore Tokyo

ISBN 978-1-349-03301-0   ISBN 978-1-349-03299-0 (eBook)
DOI 10.1007/978-1-349-03299-0

To Barbara

Contents

List of Tables and Figures

Introduction

In the last few years the growing significance of the Middle East in the international economy has been highlighted in the financial press, with articles appearing almost daily about massive new trade deals concluded with particular countries. Despite this attention, no comprehensive study has been made of the external economic relations of the region as a whole. It was this gap that prompted the author to write this book, which attempts to analyse recent trends in Middle Eastern trade and investment and to consider their implications, both for the region itself, and for the world at large. The work should also serve to put current developments in historical perspective, by providing background information on import and export trade, as well as on capital movements.

In Chapter 1 the region's resources are reviewed, including manpower and capital supplies, which helps to explain how trade patterns have evolved. The second chapter concentrates on trade in primary agricultural produce, of paramount importance historically and still significant today. As elsewhere in the Third World, prices for primary produce from the Middle East are subject to severe fluctuations, thus making the main cash crop producers extremely vulnerable to world market conditions. Seeking to overcome this problem and reduce dependence on imported manufactured goods, most governments in the area have instigated policies of import substitution, as outlined in Chapter 3. Ironically, however, this may increase the total import bill because of the need for costly foreign capital equipment, as the case studies of Egypt and Iran illustrate. Nevertheless, the following chapter's discussion shows how import duties still do protect infant domestic industries and how exchange rate policies raise the level of protection even further.

The growth of intra-regional trade is considered in Chapter 5, which includes an evaluation of the Arab Common Market, whose record to date has proved disappointing despite the optimism of the original treaty. This chapter also contains an assessment of the financial transfers within the region and their economic impact, and a critical account of the operation of the Kuwait Fund for Arab Economic Development, the longest-established Arab aid organisation. In the concluding chapter the economic links of the Middle East with the outside world are examined, with detailed information provided on export and import volumes, as well as prices. Capital flows both to and from the region are analysed, including the question of oil revenue recycling. This topical issue is perhaps best considered last, as so much of the study has a bearing on it.

In preparing this work I owe a debt of gratitude to Dr Dick Lawless, the head of the Middle East Documentation Centre in Durham, for the help he has given me in collecting material. I would also like to thank Professors Walter Elkan and Denis O'Brien of the Department of Economics in Durham for their encouragement with my research over the years and for the time they have spent discussing Middle Eastern work. In addition, I must acknowledge the help of those I met in the Middle East, too numerous to mention, both for the way they have stimulated my thinking and for the warm hospitality they have shown during my frequent visits; and I wish to thank Durham University, and its Middle East Travel Fund, for making those visits possible. Last, but by no means least, I would like to thank Lovaine Ord for the long hours spent typing out and correcting the manuscript.

1 The Factor Endowment

According to the classical theory of international trade, countries specialise in producing those goods in which they have a comparative advantage over their competitors, and then obtain their other commodity requirements by exchanging domestically produced goods for imports which they are not able to produce economically themselves. Historically the trade of the countries of the Middle East has tended to conform to this pattern, although, increasingly, government regulation of economic affairs has meant that the trade flows predicted by classical *laissez-faire* models have tended to be distorted. A country's comparative advantage in the production of a particular commodity is of course determined by what is usually referred to as its 'factor endowment', or in other words, the local availability of resources such as labour, agricultural land, mineral resources, capital or technology. Thus, for example, Egypt which has abundant cheap labour, and a good supply of fertile irrigated land, has specialised in cotton production for which its climate is well suited, and for over a century has traded cotton exports for imports of manufactured goods.[1] Similarly, for hundreds of years Iran has specialised in carpet production, with the skilled weavers of Tabriz and Isfahan using local wool from the mountains. Neighbouring Iraq has specialised in dates, while in North Yemen the main export has been coffee. Lebanon specialises in fruit and vegetables, while Israel since its inception as a state has built up a flourishing trade in citrus fruit. The Middle East therefore provides numerous illustrations of trade based on comparative advantage, with countries usually exporting those goods which their factor endowments are best suited to provide at low cost.

For the last thirty years, the main export of the Middle East has been oil. As the region accounts for over 60 per cent of world oil reserves, and 40 per cent of current oil production,[2] resources are such that trade can be justified from a mercantilist standpoint alone, as it provides a 'vent for a surplus'.[3] There is no need to explain trade in petroleum in terms of comparative, or even absolute advantage, even though the Middle East has both as far as oil production costs are concerned. The region as a whole produces over fourteen times the amount of oil it consumes, but production levels can be maintained at minimal opportunity cost to the major exporting countries, as little local labour or capital is used in extraction, so production in the non-oil sector does not suffer from any redeployment of resources into oil. Given these minimal opportunity costs in oil production, the Middle East producers may as well maintain production at as high a level as optimal depletion policies merit, balancing conservation considerations against foreign exchange needs. It would be inappropriate therefore to consider oil production in the Middle East as a specialisation, comparable in an economic sense to Egyptian cotton or Persian carpets, as the resource endowment is such that there are no economically viable alternative modes of production in which those factors engaged in oil production could be employed. It is ironic that trade in a commodity as vital to modern society as oil should be explained in terms of a theory associated with pre-industrial times, which predates even Adam Smith or David Ricardo, although in the Middle East context it is perhaps fitting that mercantilist ideas are applicable.

Whether the 'vent for a surplus theory', or 'comparative advantage' is used to explain trade, it seems clear that it is only through an understanding of the factor endowment of the Middle East, that its current trade patterns can be comprehended, the scope for widening trade assessed, and future trends predicted. In a country with abundant labour resources but capital scarcity, such as Egypt for example, it would be foolish to believe that any industry using capital rather than labour intensive productive processes could be competitive in international markets.[4] Similarly in Kuwait or Libya, the lack of local technological expertise means that the introduction of modern sophisticated industrial plants seems inappropriate given the limited local markets, and the doubtful export prospects, unless finished products are of a high standard. The economic viability of some of the high cost agricultural projects being undertaken by the oil-rich states seems even more doubtful, given the unpromising desert environment, the lack of experience with settled agriculture, and the high costs of water provision. In areas such as the Gulf, in so far as the principles of comparative advantage are valid, it would be more beneficial to import agricultural produce from countries such as Iraq, where the factor endowment is suited to agriculture, than to attempt to achieve even a measure of local self-sufficiency.

A country's factor endowment is significant for investment as well as trade. The domestic availability of the required factors of production must be taken into account when an appraisal is made of any investment project. Saudi Arabia is, for example, undertaking huge investments in new industry in an effort to diversify economic activity under the country's most recent 5-year plan.[5] Given present manpower shortages, and the kingdom's limited population, variously estimated at 4 to 9 million, it seems unlikely that sufficient local personnel will be available to staff the new factories. Even the planners admit that by 1980 migrant workers from Yemen and elsewhere will account for at least 50 per cent of the industrial workforce, which could result in severe social strains. In the Middle East where economic, social and political factors are closely interrelated, the prospective investor must take account of all these possible ramifications of any new project. Most governments in the region are keen to modernise their economies, and use the most up-to-date techniques. Intermediate technology is consequently considered second best, even where it is more suited to the local endowment. Yet as the experience of Syria and Iraq shows, a shortage of experienced managers can result in new industries facing severe teething problems once sophisticated plants are placed in local hands,[6] despite the fact that both these countries have well established secondary and higher education systems.

Consideration of the factor endowment of the Middle East as a whole, and intra-regional variations in factor availability, seems an appropriate starting point for a study of trade and investment. As the rate of population growth in the long run determines the supply of labour, this is considered first, as the most important variable influencing the factor endowment equation.

DEMOGRAPHIC TRENDS

The rate of population increase in the Middle East is higher than that found in any other region of the Third World, except for Latin America. Not only is the population growth rate high, but it is apparently accelerating as Table 1.1 shows. During 1958–63, the weighted average rate of increase for the 14 largest states in the region was 2·64 per cent. By 1963–71 the rate had risen to 2·81 per cent.[7]

There is considerable inter-country variation in the rate of increase. The exceptionally high figure for Kuwait does not indicate natural increase, but rather the immigration of large numbers of other Arabs,

TABLE 1.1. Population growth in the Middle East

Country	1963 ('000)	1971 ('000)	Rate of increase 1958–63	Rate of increase 1963–71	Population density (1971)
Turkey	29,655	36,162	2·9	2·5	46
Egypt	27,947	34,130	2·5	2·5	34
Iran	23,427	29,783	2·4	3·0	18
Iraq	7554	9750	1·6	3·2	22
Saudi Arabia	6416	7965	1·9	2·7	4
Syria	4989	6451	4·2	3·3	35
Yemen	4753	5900	2·6	2·7	30
Israel	2376	3013	3·5	3·0	146
Lebanon	2278	2873	3·0	2·9	276
Jordan	1823	2383	2·9	3·4	24
Libya	1504	2010	3·7	3·7	1
South Yemen	1164	1475	3·1	3·0	5
Kuwait	394	831	10·7	9·8	47
Oman	535	678	0·5	3·0	3
Average rate of increase for the area weighted by population size			2·64	2·81	

Note: Rate of population change calculated by

$$r = \left(\sqrt[t]{\frac{P_1}{P_0}} - 1 \right)100$$

P_0 is population in base year 1963 or 1958.
P_1 is population in the final year 1971 or 1963.
t is the time between base and final periods, 5 or 8 years.
Sources: U.N., *Demographic Yearbooks*, 1964 and 1971.

attracted by the employment opportunities made possible by the country's enormous oil revenues. The reliability of some of the country estimates is also open to question. For example, the recorded rate of increase in Syria for the 1958–63 period is unbelievably high, yet it cannot be accounted for by immigration, which is negligible in Syria. The maximum rate of increase usually reckoned as biologically possible is well under 4 per cent. Though, however, there are undoubtedly discrepancies existing in the figures for some countries, these may not affect the overall average as much as might be expected. It is the data from the smaller countries which is most unreliable, rather than that from the larger countries which have longer experiences with census taking. As the average is weighted by population size, the significance of the errors is reduced when considering the region as a whole.

To what factors can this accelerating rate of population increase be attributed? From Table 1.2 it emerges that birth-rate changes cannot

TABLE 1.2. Changes in Middle Eastern birth rates and fertility rates

	Crude birth rates		Fertility rates	
	1967	1971	1967	1971
Turkey	43·0	39·6	—	—
Egypt	39·3	34·9	150·3	150·3
Iran	48·0	45·4	161·5	161·8
Iraq	(17·8)	(49·3)	(39·8)	(60·5)
Saudi Arabia	—	50·0	—	—
Syria	(32·1)	(47·5)	(125·7)	(126·3)
North Yemen	—	50·0	—	—
Israel	25·5	26·8	89·5	95·2
Lebanon	31·2	26·5	—	—
Jordan	47·0	49·1	170·5	169·7
Libya	(25·1)	(45·9)	(101·2)	—
Kuwait	51·6	43·3	220·7	190·0
Average rates for area weighted by population size (excluding countries whose figures are bracketed)	42·5	39·3	153·6	153·9

Sources: U.N., *Demographic Yearbooks*, 1967 and 1971.

be held responsible. In the major Middle East countries, Turkey, Egypt and Iran, these rates appear to be falling. A weighted average of the seven countries in the area with the most reliable data confirms this trend, with the birth rate declining from 42·5 live births per 1000 population to 39·3. Figures for Iraq, Syria and Libya are excluded from this average, as their estimates for 1967 seem dubiously low.

It is interesting to note that though birth rates are falling, this decrease is not reflected in fertility rates. The latter refer to the number of live births reported in the calendar year per 1000 female population aged 10–49 years. If fertility rates are relatively constant while birth rates are falling, this indicates a change in the age structure of the population.

In the Middle East, given the population trends of the previous decade, this structural change partly reflects the increase in the child population. However, as there has also been an increase in life expectancy due to improved health measures, the proportion of those in older age groups above child-bearing age has also expanded. Changes in the age structure will affect the ratio of those of working age to those in the total population. If the 'dependency burden' is altered in this way, there will clearly be economic implications. More will be said about this later.

If the birth rate is not responsible for the rapid population increase in the Middle East, then it follows that changes in the death rate must be the main factor. Table 1.3 shows how the death rate has declined in

TABLE 1.3. Changes in Middle Eastern death rates and infant mortality rates

	Crude death rates		Infant mortality	
	1967	1971	1967	1971
Turkey	16·0	14·6	161·0	153·0
Egypt	14·3	15·0	(83·2)	(119.0)
Iran	24·5	16·6	—	—
Iraq	(3·9)	(15·5)	17·9	16·2
Saudi Arabia	—	22·7	—	—
Syria	(4·5)	(15·3)	28·1	24·5
Yemen	—	22·7	—	—
Israel	6·3	7·0	25·3	22·9
Lebanon	4·6	4·5	13·6	13·6
Jordan	16·0	16·0	36·3	36·3
Libya	(4·1)	(15·8)	—	—
Kuwait	5·7	7·4	37·0	39·4
Average rate for area weighted by population size (excluding countries whose figures are bracketed)	17·6	15·6	97·2	105·5

Sources: U.N., *Demographic Yearbooks*, 1967 and 1971.

both Turkey and Iran. In Egypt there has been a downward trend for the last two decades, but after 1967 there was a slight rise. This can be attributed to the aftermath of the Six Day War, which was a period of considerable disruption due to the necessity of evacuating the canal cities because of continuing hostilities. The temporary increase in the infant mortality rate was due to the problems of providing adequate health facilities for the refugees. As with the birth-rate figures, the death rates given for Iraq, Syria and Libya during 1967 need to be treated with scepticism.

In the higher-income countries of the area, death rates and infant mortality rates were much lower, as can be seen from the figures for Lebanon, Israel and Kuwait. With development therefore, and provision of improved health and hospital facilities, further dramatic declines in death rates and infant mortality rates can be expected in the major Middle East countries. Unless there is an accompanying decline in birth rates and fertility rates, present trends will result in the population of the region doubling inside 20 years.

POPULATION GROWTH AND THE LABOUR FORCE

There will clearly be a long-run relationship between the growth of population and the size of the labour force. On this time scale these additions to the labour force will have a positive effect from the point of view of output growth, provided the marginal productivity of labour is positive. Of course in so far as there is underemployment of the existing workforce, and the marginal productivity of labour approaches zero, the contribution of additional labour to productivity may be minimal. Thus where factors complementary to labour are in short supply, as is the case of capital and land in parts of the Middle East, additions to the workforce may do little to improve production supplies.

In the Middle East it seems doubtful, however, that this is the reality in practice. Egypt, for example, was long regarded as a classic example of this zero marginal productivity case. Though Egypt remains primarily agrarian its population density exceeds that of most of the industrialised countries of Western Europe. Recently, however, strong evidence has become available to support the view that labour's marginal product is positive even in Egypt.[8] A major survey in the mid-1960s of rural employment revealed that in peak harvest periods, there were actually labour shortages in Egypt in agriculture, and that any underemployment that existed in Egypt was highly seasonal.[9] In addition wages appeared to fluctuate seasonally, with the peaks of the cycle coinciding with the periods when labour shortages existed.[10] With demand factors operative in Egyptian wage determination, labour's marginal product is well above zero.

The contribution of population growth to output will not be immediate. There will be a considerable lag in fact before there is any impact on production, as people are usually at least 15 years of age before they enter the workforce in a full-time capacity. In the Middle East, however, there is a certain amount of child labour, so people may make some contribution to production at an earlier age. Usually in practice this help involves work at peak harvest periods, but this is important as it helps relieve any labour bottlenecks.

Though the effect of population increase on output supply is likely to be zero in the short run, owing to the lag before the workforce is augmented, the effect on the demand side is immediate. More people means increased demand for food, clothing, housing, consumer durables and services. Children's needs for some of these items such as food are admittedly smaller, but for clothing and services they are probably greater.

One feature of the population structure of most Middle Eastern states is the very high dependency burden. This can be assessed by comparing the numbers of dependent non-workers (children, the aged) to those engaged actively in the workforce. If population increase were reduced, the lower resulting dependency burden would mean that everyone could be better off, and per capita incomes could rise. With little change in the volume of production available, but fewer people in the market on the demand side, per capita consumption can obviously be higher.[11]

The dependency burden can be illustrated in terms of the age profiles of a country's population. Those for Turkey, Egypt and Iran are illustrated in Figure 1. In the Middle Eastern states, over 40 per cent of the population is in the under-15 age group. Hence the age profiles are pyramid-shaped. In developed countries in contrast the proportion in the younger age group is much lower, and hence the base of the pyramid is narrower.

Though developed countries have a lower number of dependants under 15, this favourable effect on dependency may be partly offset by having a larger proportion in the older age groups. This offsetting factor is not as great, however, as is frequently imagined. Life expectancies in developed and developing countries do not differ so much once people have survived infancy. Thus, for example, in Egypt a girl aged 20 can expect to live a further 53 years. In the United Kingdom the same girl could expect to survive a further 56 years, only 3 years more. As most of the workforce survives into old age in the Middle East, this implies the slope of the sides of the age pyramid is largely a function of birth rates and infant mortality rates until the 60s age group at least.

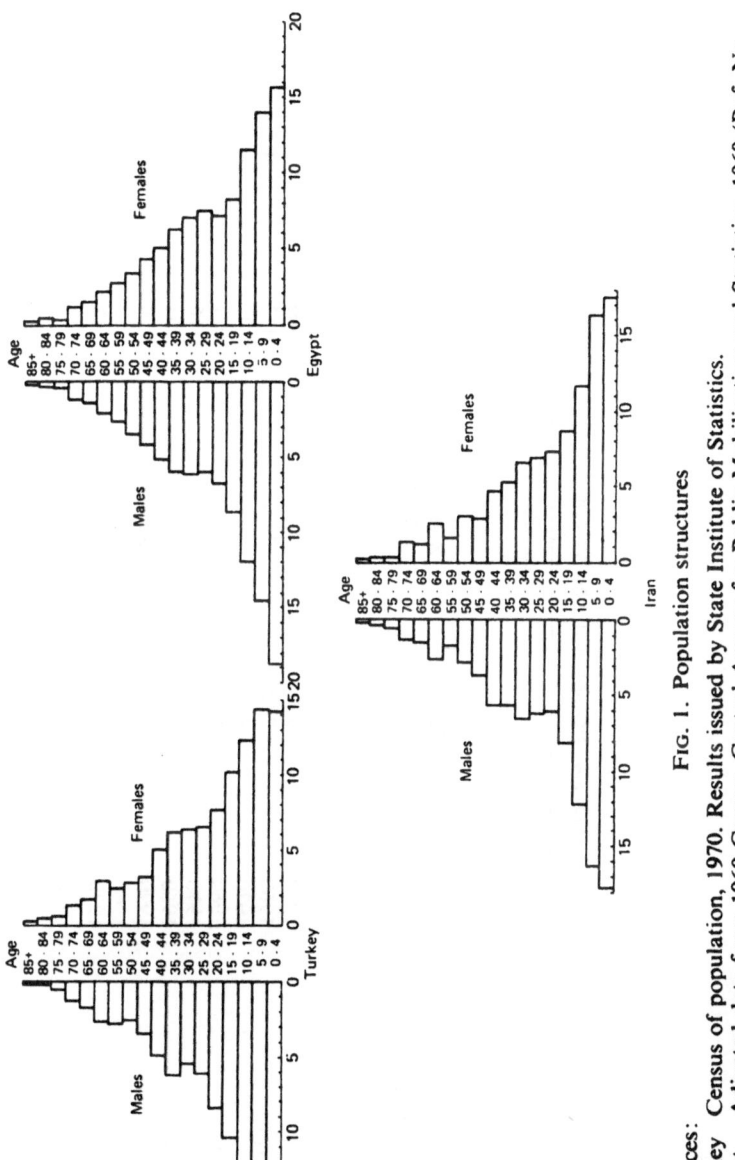

FIG. 1. Population structures

Sources:
Turkey Census of population, 1970. Results issued by State Institute of Statistics.
Egypt   Adjusted data from 1960 Census, Central Agency for Public Mobilisation and Statistics, 1969 (Ref. No. 05–100).
Iran   Census data from Plan Organisation 1966 Vol. 168. Cited by B. D. Clarke, Iran, Changing Population Patterns in J. I. Clarke and W. B. Fisher (eds.), *Populations of the Middle East and North Africa* (University of London Press, 1972).

TABLE 1.4. Economically active population

Country	Year	Economically Active Population			
		Total ('000)	% total population	In agriculture ('000)	% In agriculture to total economically active
Turkey	1960	13,255	48·2	10,357	78·2
	1970	15,548	44·8	11,014	69·1
Iran	1960	6389	29·7	3443	53·9
	1970	7794	27·5	3609	46·3
Egypt	1960	7379	28·6	4313	58·4
	1970	9174	27·1	5023	54·7
Iraq	1960	1839	26·5	977	53·1
	1970	2395	24·7	1116	46·6
Jordan	1960	442	26·1	194	43·9
	1970	564	24·3	218	38·6
Kuwait	1960	117	42·1	2	1·7
	1970	282	39·7	3	1·1

Lebanon	1960	586	27·8	310	52·9
	1970	732	26·3	347	47·4
Libya	1960	381	27·4	211	55·4
	1970	513	26·0	219	42·7
Israel	1960	756	35·8	109	14·4
	1970	1059	36·5	111	10·5
Saudi Arabia	1960	1724	28·8	1232	71·5
	1970	2109	27·2	1276	60·5
Sudan	1960	3888	33·0	3333	85·7
	1970	5065	32·1	4046	79·9
Syria	1960	1263	27·7	685	54·2
	1970	1574	25·5	768	48·8
North Yemen	1960	1357	30·6	1128	83·1
	1970	1689	29·5	1238	73·3
South Yemen	1960	285	28·8	201	70·5
	1970	347	27·1	216	62·2

Source: FAO, *Production Yearbook*, 1972, Table 5, p. 21.

The high dependency burden in the Middle East is reflected in the figures for the proportion of the population economically active, as shown in Table 1.4. The proportion of the population economically active is below one-third in many countries of the area, and in no country does it exceed 40 per cent. It is interesting to note that the proportion is actually falling in the vast majority of countries, which reflects the high rates of population increase. Care must be exercised in using this data, however, as the figures for the economically active population refer only to those in enumerated employment, but a large proportion of the workforce, especially those engaged in agriculture, are not taken account of in the official statistics. Many are employed on a casual basis, at peak harvesting seasons only, as already mentioned. In countries such as Egypt, where employers are obliged to make welfare contributions to the state for the benefit of their employees, there may be a reluctance to register all employees, and a large number work on a self-employed basis, which is much cheaper for employers.

The higher proportion shown to be in the economically active population in city states such as Kuwait may merely reflect the absence of an agricultural sector, and the fact that most people in services or industry tend to be in registered employment. Few women are registered as being in the economically active population, especially in the more conservative Muslim states such as Saudi Arabia where women are largely confined to the home. Even in countries where women have more freedom and many girls are highly educated, as is the case in Egypt, the proportion of women in the economically active workforce is below 10 per cent. That is not to say that women do not undertake a significant amount of work in the Middle East. Usually they undertake most of the work in the home, and often, as in the Lebanon or Tunisia, a large part of the work in agriculture, but this is not registered in the official statistics. The data presented in Table 1.4 therefore seriously underestimates the actual workforce, and even inter-country comparisons can be misleading; but the data at least gives an approximate indication of the proportions involved.

In every country of the region the proportion of the economically active population engaged in agriculture is falling, although in many countries the absolute numbers in agricultural employment are still rising as a consequence of rural population growth, even despite high migration into urban areas from the countryside.[12] Most of the main agricultural countries of the region have still over half of their total workforce engaged in agriculture, despite the decline by an average of 5 per cent in most cases during the decade from 1960 to 1970. As much of the new industry established in the Middle East in recent years has been capital intensive, there has been little redeployment from agriculture into industry. Even in Egypt, the country with the most well established industrial bases in the whole Arab world, the proportion of the enumerated workforce engaged in industrial activity amounts to only 15 per cent. There, as elsewhere, the fastest-growing sector has been services, which accounts for over a quarter of the total population in wage employment. The government bureaucracies have steadily increased in size in most countries of the area in recent years, despite serious overmanning and low productivity. In one sense these employees can barely be considered economically active. An increasing number of people are engaged in trading activity, which also accounts for some of the increase in the size of the service sector. The official statistics, however, tend to underestimate the extent of the service sector, as those in unenumerated occupations such as street vendors or domestic servants are not included, yet they are numerous in the Middle East.

AVAILABILITY OF CAPITAL

The rapidly increasing population of the Middle East cannot make a contribution to output unless it is accompanied by a high level of capital formation. Although the region as a whole is relatively well endowed with capital resources, as a consequence of its oil revenues, there are considerable variations from country to country. Saudi Arabia, for example, receives more oil revenue than any other state in the Middle East, a situation which is likely to continue as its oil reserves account for almost half the area's total. As a consequence of the huge increase in oil revenues which resulted from the January 1974 oil price increases, the country has embarked on a new £60,000 million development plan to modernise its economy. The development plan of oil-rich Iran is the largest and most ambitious in the Middle East, as it aims at raising the living standards of the country's 33 million people to a level comparable to that of Western Europe by the 1980s.[13] Investment projects are being undertaken to diversify the economy, with the emphasis on the promotion of manufacturing activity.

The oil revenue boom has benefited not only rich oil producers, such as Iran and Saudi Arabia, but also poorer Middle Eastern states with teeming populations but few mineral resources, such as Egypt. During 1975 alone Egypt has received almost £30 million for the modernisation and expansion of its railway system from the Saudi Development Fund

and a similar sum to finance a new urban highway linking the Cairo
suburb of Heliopolis with the steel town of Helwan. Such aid yields
political rather than economic dividends for the Saudis, especially as
Egypt has always been at the centre of pan-Arab politics and is the
country most critically involved in the dispute with Israel. To encourage
Arab oil revenue into investments in Egypt, the government launched
a new open-door policy. This provides for 5-year tax holidays for all
new investment, and free remission of profits. It is hoped to channel
Arab money into free zones being created in the Suez Canal area where
new industrial complexes are being planned.[14]

Almost all the poorer Arab states have benefited to some degree from
aid received through the Kuwait Fund for Arab Economic Development, with low interest loans provided to finance agricultural as well as
industrial projects.[15] Countries such as Syria and Egypt have received
substantial amounts, with the latter helped with the financing of the reopening of the Suez Canal. Both Syria and Egypt have also received
large sums of aid from the Soviet Union, though much of this has been
for the purchase of military equipment rather than civilian projects.
The Soviet Union has during the last decade channelled almost three-
quarters of its total overseas aid to the Middle East region alone, in-
dicating the country's keen interest in the area. Western aid has been
less significant in the Arab world, although individual countries like
Jordan, for example, have obtained substantial amounts in relation to
the size of their economies. Most United States aid goes to one country
in the area—Israel—which incredibly now receives almost two-thirds
of America's total overseas grants according to one recent estimate.

The uneven distribution of the oil wealth of the Middle East is indicated by Table 1.5. Iran was the largest producer until the 1970s, but
its reserves are less than half those of Saudi Arabia, which alone accounts for over 37 per cent of the total reserves of the Middle East, and
over one-quarter of the total non-communist world's reserves. Given
Saudi Arabia's limited labour supply, and its harsh desert environment,
the economy's capacity to absorb the oil revenue is very limited. Saudi
Arabia may feel tempted to safeguard its future by leaving its oil in the
ground to ensure a supply of reserves for as long ahead as possible.
Kuwait with only 1 million people, half of whom are immigrants anyway, is in a similar position, and is only utilising its reserves slowly, so
that it can maintain oil production for over 60 years at present levels.[16]
It is interesting to note that oil production in Kuwait actually contracted
slightly over the 1969–74 period, even before the worldwide recession
in demand for petroleum products following the 1974 price rises.

TABLE 1.5. Oil reserves, production and revenues for major Middle Eastern producers

	Proven reserves in 1973				Production (thousand barrels a day)		Revenue (million U.S.$) 1974
	Million barrels	% of total Middle East reserves	% of total non-communist world reserves	No. of years production at 1973 levels	1969	1974	
Iran	60,000	17·1	11·4	28	3376	6022	21,443
Iraq	31,500	9·0	6·0	43	1521	1975	5046*
Kuwait	64,000	18·2	12·2	63	2773	2546	1805
Libya	34,100	9·4	5·8	43	1521	3109	2243
Oman	5250	1·5	1·0	49	50	380	971*
Qatar	6500	1·8	1·2	31	355	518	1541
Saudi Arabia	132,000	37·7	25·1	49	3216	8480	23,195
U.A.E.	4360	1·1	0·8	30	628	1679	4290*

Sources: Reserves—*Oil and Gas Journal.*
Production—OPEC, *Annual Statistics Bulletin,* 1975.
Notes: * Approximate conversions at $7 a barrel government take.

Those oil-producing nations with only limited domestic absorptive capacities have used their surplus revenue to finance overseas investment, mostly in the main financial centres of the West. However, as a consequence of the uncertainties in Western stock markets, and the fluctuations in exchange rates resulting from the floating of currencies, Arab investors are reluctant to undertake long-term investments in stocks and shares, apart from property investment, which is felt to be a better security. Instead, assets are held in the form of short-term demand deposits with just a few big American and European banks.[17] These earn only low interest yields, however, and in practice the real value of interest earnings has been negative over the last few years when inflation is taken into account. Oil-producing nations have not been able to benefit, even when funds are placed in countries with strong currencies such as Switzerland, where interest rates on deposit accounts involving large amounts have actually been negative, which more than offsets any gains from currency appreciation.

As a result of these problems in safeguarding the value of their financial assets, the oil-producing nations have not been as disappointed by the worldwide fall in demand for petroleum during the mid-1970s as might have been expected. The oil-producing nations of the Gulf and Saudi Arabia have become increasingly conservation-minded, especially as they have great confidence in the ability of Organisation of Petroleum Exporting Countries (OPEC) to maintain high prices. Since the nationalisation of the Western companies operating oil concessions, the Middle East producers have strengthened their position, as they can now control production levels. In oil production, an international cartel has replaced the corporate oligopoly, with the nations involved having a guaranteed rental income, which they can protect through controlling supplies. The less populous countries with lower foreign exchange requirements can easily decrease production in response to changes in world demand, and Kuwait exercised this option in 1975, when reductions amounted to 37 per cent, while Libyan production was down by almost half. Saudi Arabia could pay for its current import requirements with less than half its present level of oil production. By May 1975 the kingdom's holdings of gold and foreign exchange were greater than those of the United States.[18]

Countries such as Iran are in a different position however, as their oil revenue requirements are much greater. The volume of investment funds needed to diversify the economy of this populous country is considerable and, during the period of the current 1973–78 plan alone, it is expected that investments worth over $20,000 million will be undertaken.

This compares with an expenditure of under $600 million during the last plan period, two-thirds of which was financed from oil revenue. Projected oil revenues by the end of the decade in Iran will just keep pace with financial needs and, although following the 1974 price increases there were some surplus funds which were placed in overseas investment holdings, this is rapidly disappearing, and some planned domestic investments are even being cut back. The Iranian authorities are therefore running petroleum production at a high level, as indicated in Table 1.5, despite the fact that reserves are the least adequate in relation to current production of all the Middle Eastern oil exporters. It is hoped, however, that long before the oil revenues run out, Iran's infant industries will have reached maturity, and they will be able to compete successfully in export markets themselves, thus offering an alternative to crude petroleum and petroleum products as a source of foreign exchange earnings.[19]

Despite the present emphasis on investment in Iran, gross fixed capital formation has not been high in the past in relation to G.N.P., as Table 1.6 shows. Gross fixed capital formation was higher for example in non-oil-exporting states such as Turkey, Jordan or Syria in 1972, and yet this was not a year when disruption caused any abnormalities. Surprisingly, Iraq and Saudi Arabia also exhibit low rates of capital formation in relation to the other states cited in the table. These findings can be explained partly by the fact that investment finance may not be the critical constraint on capital formation, but rather investment opportunities. In Saudi Arabia and Kuwait, for example, opportunities to diversify the economy through profitable investment are limited, for reasons already discussed. Even basic infrastructure can only be built up slowly, in a country such as Saudi Arabia, as there is not the labour to do the work, or even port facilities adequate to cope with large consignments of imported building materials and machinery.

The nature of the economic activity in the major oil-producing nations may also explain the low level of capital formation until recently. Basic infrastructure is, not surprisingly, usually only developed when there is a need for it in order to extend profitable economic activity. For example, in Egypt in the nineteenth century, the anticipated payoff from cotton production was so great that road and rail links were developed rapidly so that cotton could be transported to the port of Alexandria and onwards to the textile factories of Europe. With oil production, however, once the drilling equipment is installed and the pipelines and tanker terminals are constructed, there is little need for further infrastructure. It is cheaper for the petroleum companies to purchase

TABLE 1.6. Capital formation and output in the Middle East

	Gross domestic product			Gross fixed capital formation		
	Level, 1972 (million U.S.$)	Per capita, 1972 (U.S.$)	Growth 1960–72 (%)	% of G.N.P. (1972)	Growth 1964–70 (%)	Growth 1970–73 (%)
Turkey	13,650	370	3·9	18·0	8·2	4·4
Egypt	8340	240	1·5	12·6	−1·9	0·8
Iran	15,220	490	6·3	14·1	12·2	23·1
Iraq	3730	370	2·7	13·1	N/A	10·9
Saudi Arabia	4160	550	7·2	12·3	N/A	53·2
Syria	2150	320	3·4	19·9	8·8	7·0
Yemen	550	90	2·0	12·2	N/A	27·1
Israel	8050	2610	5·7	N/A	5·3	13·6
Lebanon	2030	700	1·0	19·1	N/A	14·4
Jordan	670	270	1·7	23·8	N/A	2·5
Libya	3820	830	16·2	19·0	14·0	3·6
Kuwait	3440	4090	−2·1	10·4	N/A	2·4

Sources: Gross domestic product data—*World Bank Atlas*, Washington, 1974.
Capital formation—*The Arab World: Key Indicators*, Kuwait Fund for Arab Economic Development, April 1975. U.N., *Monthly Bulletin of Statistics*, December 1975. U.N., *Statistical Yearbook*, 1974. I.M.F., *International Financial Statistics*, December 1975.

four-wheel drive vehicles than improve the local roads. Therefore in Saudi Arabia and the Gulf, there was little trunk road construction until recent years, and only small amounts of spending on port facilities for general cargoes. Hence the low level of domestic gross fixed capital formation in these areas. Recently, however, as the producing nations' share of oil proceeds has risen, and domestic purchasing power subsequently increased, the need for facilities to distribute imports has arisen. It is this that explains the rapid growth of gross fixed capital formation over the most recent period for which figures are available, 1970–73, as indicated in Table 1.6. In one sense, what has been occurring in Saudi Arabia or Iran is the opposite of what happened earlier in Egypt. In the latter, infrastructure was developed to take the exports out, while in the former, the oil-rich states, it is being built up to bring in the imports.

Political instability may also have an adverse effect on gross fixed capital formation. In countries such as Iraq where governments have changed frequently since the revolution of 1958 that overthrew the monarchy, there has been no stable constitution, and each new government has meant the replacement of many of the senior civil servants and planners. The economic climate has been adversely affected by the continuing conflict with the Kurds, whose claimed homelands lie dangerously close to the country's oilfields. There has been a considerable diversion of resources from civilian to military purposes, which has seriously harmed the economy.[20] Even the present government has described the 1960–70 period as a decade of wasted opportunity. In Egypt, although the post-revolutionary period has been much more stable politically, the long confrontation with Israel, and the two major open conflicts, have left their mark on the economy. Gross capital formation actually declined as a proportion of gross national product over the 1964–70 period as Table 1.6 shows. There was scarcely any growth in the rate of investment, even over the more recent 1970–73 period, as massive arms purchases continued. For a poor country such as Egypt, whose per capita income only amounts to $240, the opportunity cost of conflict has clearly been enormous in terms of development forgone.

Although capital formation is one of the main determinants of economic growth, the relationship is complex, as other factors such as the rate of population increase and the level of technology are also critical. There would appear to be no clear association between the level of capital formation and the level of gross national product in the main countries of the Middle East, as the data presented in Table 1.6 confirms. Nor is there any relationship between the growth of these two variables.

The major oil-exporting nations exhibit the highest levels of per capita income, as might be expected; but apart from Libya, none have particularly high rates of gross fixed capital formation, basically because of the reasons already discussed. It is interesting to note that in Kuwait, the country with the highest per capita income, there was actually a contraction over the 1960–72 period as a whole, although this trend has been reversed in recent years. The high level of immigration into the country was the prime cause of this contraction: a rate of population increase averaging almost 10 per cent more than offset any income increases.

Data on gross domestic product can be a very misleading indicator of development however, even when presented on a per capita basis.[21] The figures given in Table 1.6 would suggest that Libya, for example, is almost three times as developed as Egypt, but this type of inter-country comparison is virtually meaningless. Egypt's low per capita level of domestic product merely reflects its large population; although living standards are admittedly poor for the majority of the country's people, the economy is nevertheless highly diversified. Today Egypt can boast the most advanced industrial sector in the entire Arab world, with manufacturing production ranging from consumer durables to iron and steel. Libya, in contrast, is dependent on one resource, oil, and is a classic case of a dual economy, with few external linkages between the oil sector and the remainder of the economy.[22] In terms of human resources, Egypt is also well endowed, with a larger proportion of its population receiving higher education than in many European countries, even though the quality of education may not be as high. Education expansion in Libya, in contrast, has been very recent, and large numbers, even of the younger people, remain illiterate nomads.

The quadrupling of oil prices in January 1974, and the consequent effect on income of the oil-exporting nations, has meant that the figures relating to those countries in Table 1.6 seriously underestimate current levels of per capita income. As a complete set of data is not available for the countries covered for a later period, it is not possible to make a more recent comparison. The magnitude of the effect of the oil price increases can be gauged from the data for Saudi Arabia whose per capita income now stands at over $2900, almost the same level as that of the United Kingdom. This increase, however, only serves to highlight the inadequacy of using such data as an indicator of development. More will be said about this point when discussing indicators of market strength in the final chapter of this study.

Despite the arid desert environment of most of the land area of the

Middle East, this review of the area's human and capital resources shows that the region has been generously endowed. The major difference between the Middle East and other regions lies in the degree of preparatory work which is necessary in order to actually bring the resources into productive use. A considerable amount of irrigation work was necessary to transform Egypt into one of the world's main sources of high-grade cotton in the nineteenth century, but there was plenty of labour available to undertake the work. Similarly, in more recent times a large amount of investment was needed in order to exploit the Middle East's rich oil resources, although as already mentioned this did not involve much reallocation of domestic resources as most of the capital came from outside the region. Today considerable effort is still needed if the region is to progress as a whole economically. The main problem for the Middle East is not one of lack of resources, for the area has vast financial resources at its disposal as well as rich human resources. For the region's planners, the greatest problem is to bring these resources together, to harness the finance and labour available for productive activity. It seems strange that the region as a whole should have so few investment opportunities, despite the extent of its population. There is a tragic waste when under-utilised capital and underemployed labour exist side by side; yet this is the situation which occurs in the Middle East. In the chapters which follow, an attempt will be made to explain this paradox. First, however, it is necessary to look at Middle Eastern agriculture as this was the main source of traditional economic activity. It is also the sector where many of the paradoxes of the region's development are most evident.

2 Trade and Development of the Agrarian Economy

The last 20 years have witnessed probably greater changes in the agricultural sector than any other single period in the history of the Middle East. Massive land reforms have been instigated in Egypt, Syria, Iraq and Iran, involving the breaking up of large estates and their redistribution to tenants, sharecroppers and farm labourers. Co-operative organisations have been set up to provide farmers with agricultural credit and farm inputs while, in addition, an increasing proportion of farm produce has been marketed through these organisations rather than the traditional merchants. New large-scale irrigation projects based, in most cases, on the experience of the Tennessee Valley Authority, have been undertaken, often with foreign assistance, to increase the land available for cultivation and to provide power.[1]

These ambitious government-sponsored schemes to transform Middle Eastern agriculture have played their part in encouraging increases in farm output. Average agricultural production has increased by over 50 per cent since the early 1950s, although there have been wide disparities between the rates of advance in different parts of the region. With population increasing at almost 3 per cent as well as increases in per capita income, this growth of output has hardly kept pace with growing food requirements, and in many Middle Eastern states, food imports and food prices have been rising sharply. In addition, with insufficient employment opportunities being created in industrial and service activities for the expanding labour force, there is undoubtedly a need for greater labour absorption in agriculture. The question discussed in this chapter is whether there is sufficient agricultural potential in the Middle East to accept these two challenges of meeting the increasing food requirements and maintaining agriculture's export contribution.

Agriculture remains the dominant economic activity throughout the Middle East, with over half the area's workforce engaged in farming.

The share of agricultural production in G.N.P. has been declining however in most countries in the region, and now it only accounts for one-quarter of G.N.P. in Egypt, Iraq, Turkey and Iran, though in Syria the proportion is higher. Despite this relative decline, agriculture remains the largest single sector in Egypt, Turkey and Syria, while in Iran and Iraq it is second after petroleum. Within the agricultural sector there has been a gradual shift away from production for subsistence with the spread of the market economy. Now most produce is marketed in the Arab world, though the greater portion of agriculture is still subsistence orientated in Iran and Turkey, with the non-monetary sector responsible for almost 60 per cent of total agricultural production in the latter country. Earnings from agriculture constitute the major source of foreign exchange, except for the major oil-producing states and Israel. In Egypt, Syria and Turkey over 60 per cent of export earnings come from agriculture, and this proportion has been declining gradually over time. This means that government policies affecting the agricultural sector are likely to have an important bearing on the economies of these countries at the macro level, as well as being of far-reaching significance at the micro level of the individual farm family. Hence the policies reviewed presently in the fields of land reform, co-operatives, agricultural credit and irrigation are of greater significance in the economic context of the Middle East than would be the case in a more developed area.

LAND REFORM

The land tenure system of the Middle East until the 1950s was characterised by an extremely uneven distribution of land ownership. Thus in Egypt, 3 per cent of the landowners possessed 55 per cent of the cultivated area, with the 60 largest owners having farms averaging almost 2000 hectares in a country where most farms were below 2 hectares in size.[2] The distribution in Iraq and Syria was even more skewed. Iraq for example had 2 per cent of its landholders owning 68 per cent of the land in cultivation.[3] Land tenure in the northern tier countries, Turkey and Iran, displayed a similar pattern. In spite of these large ownership units, there was an absence of any economies of scale in farming operations. In practice the operational units on these vast holdings were usually quite small. Often landowners were absentees, preferring to live in urban areas, and played little part in the running of their estates. Although paid managers handled the landlords' interests, the day-to-day farming operations were almost exclusively in the hands of tenants or sharecroppers. The traditional agricultural methods prevailing were in any case neutral in regard to economies in scale of operation. As few of the large landholders had invested in mechanisation schemes on their estates, serious diseconomies were unlikely to occur if 'land-to-the-tiller' reform programmes were adopted, involving reduction of the ownership unit to the size of the operational unit.

The primary motivation for land reform was political rather than economic. Those tenure reforms introduced in the Middle East in the 1950s followed political revolutions in which feudalistic oligarchies had been replaced by more radical regimes. The military uprisings causing the changes of government were essentially urban-based. A major land reform objective was to abolish the old social order in the rural areas, by attacking the positions of the large landed interests which were so powerful in the former ruling cliques. In this way it was hoped to spread the revolutions to the countryside and enlist the support of the rural people. This political factor helps to explain the speed with which land reform programmes were introduced following the revolutions in Egypt, Syria and Iraq, and the rapid pace of expropriation of large estates following the reform decrees. It also explains why in Iran, in spite of the so called 'White Revolution', implementation of land reform across the country has been slower, and why in Turkey there has been a lack of any real progress with reform during the 1960s.

The land reform laws introduced by the new Arab regimes were far reaching. Ceilings were imposed on holding size, varying from 80 hectares initially in Egypt (later reduced by half),[4] to 250 hectares in Iraq on irrigated land, and 500 hectares on rain-fed land. First priority was given to expropriation. Although land redistribution proceeded fairly rapidly in Egypt, there was a considerable lag in Syria and Iraq as Table 2.1 illustrates. There appear to be several factors explaining the delays in Syria and Iraq with redistribution.

TABLE 2.1. Scope of Middle East agrarian reforms by 1965

	Proportion of agricultural land	
	(*1*) *Expropriated*	(*2*) *Distributed*
Syria	28%	13%
Egypt	15%	12%
Iraq	42%	10%

Source: Country reports to FAO 1966 World Land Reform Conference.

(1)   Lack of reliable records of land ownership. The land surveys undertaken by the Ottomans in Iraq and Syria were outdated, and the British survey of Iraq was never comprehensive. Egypt, in contrast, had accurate land registers since the reign of Muhammad Ali in the nineteenth century, and these were kept up-to-date. In Iran this problem of land registration was overcome by using the 'village' as the basis for redistribution. Private land holding was limited to one village or its equivalent, rather than to any precise land area.

(2)   Insufficient trained staff to implement the reform. These difficulties were accentuated in Iraq and Syria where government personnel lacked the capabilities required to organise production during the period of transition between expropriation and redistribution. In Egypt these problems were much less acute, as there was a cadre of experienced agricultural officers in government service, largely as a consequence of the historically centralised control of irrigation.

(3)   A complex system of land tenure existed in Iraq and Syria, which represented a combination of traditional tribal practice, Ottoman custom and Muslim law. Although most land was nominally vested in the state, and the proportion in absolute private ownership appeared quite small, in practice the tribal sheiks were able to do as they wished with the lands they controlled, without fear of interference from the weak central administrations, except with regard to transfers in certain areas. In Egypt the system of land tenure had not been complicated to as great an extent by foreign interference, and the authorities were experienced in dealing with the intricacies of Muslim land law. Adjudication of land rights was therefore undertaken more quickly in the Nile Valley, with the land available for resettlement easier to demarcate.[6]

The amounts of land redistributed to each family were small, varying from an average of 1 hectare in Egypt, where population pressure was greatest, to 7·5–15 hectares in Iraq on irrigated land, and twice this amount in the case of lower-potential rain-fed land. In Iran the beneficiaries of the Shah's land reform probably received about 4 hectares each, although this is only a rough estimate as no accurate figures are available. In terms of potential income per holding, however, it appears that the Iranian reform programme was less generous than those undertaken in the Arab countries.[7] Although the average amount received by each family represents four times the Egyptian figure, the production potential of the fertile soils of the Nile Valley is many times greater, and hence the beneficiaries' farm income should be correspondingly larger. The production possibilities in Iran are more comparable with Iraq, yet the minimum Iraqi provision for each farm family is nearly twice as great, even on the best-irrigated land with the highest potential.

In contrast to the other states, the Syrian Government decided against direct redistribution of land to the peasants, and instead set up large co-operative farms comprising 800–1000 hectares on irrigated land, and over 1200 hectares on rain-fed land. The authorities believed that large units would facilitate mechanisation of farm operations. As part of the land reform programme those few large private farms which were already mechanised, had already been taken over and run as state farms. It was largely the favourable experience with these state enterprises which encouraged the authorities to adopt a tractorisation policy throughout all the areas brought within the scope of the land reform. These large state-managed operational units maintained the high level of grain production attained under the previous private ownership, but there is no evidence that the state farms were successful in achieving a greater intensity of land use, or in generating additional employment opportunities in agriculture. It seems doubtful if encouragement of mechanised farming on large units is the best policy for Syria. The merit of mechanisation, which means replacement of local draught animals by imported machinery, is open to question, especially when countries face a shortage of foreign exchange.[8] As only small numbers can benefit from the land reform by becoming members of the new co-operatives, many of the former tenants and sharecroppers failed to be absorbed when their plots were consolidated into larger units for mechanisation. This problem did not arise on the state farms, as these replaced large farms run on Western lines with minimal labour requirements, and hence no change in factor proportions was involved.

It was generally hoped that the new stability and security of tenure experienced by the peasants in Egypt, Iraq and Iran would provide a powerful stimulus for farm improvement. Smallholders could undertake plans to intensify their farm production, secure in the knowledge that most additional income generated would accrue to themselves and their families, apart from the portions deducted to meet loan repayments and finance marketing. Although major schemes such as irrigation and drainage works were undertaken by the state, there remained considerable scope for individual initiative. Farmers could introduce improved seed, fertiliser and insecticides, purchase better farm implements, construct farm buildings, fences and drains, and raise the quality of any animal stock kept. However, it is difficult to quantify in isolation the net effect on production of these new incentives resulting from land reform, as the governments involved introduced many other measures to help their agricultural sectors simultaneously. Nevertheless it appears that the land reforms did have a positive effect on rural incomes, which to a large extent is directly attributable to the redistribution of income from the former landlords, who often lived in urban areas as already mentioned. It has been estimated in Egypt that farm incomes during the 1950s increased by over 50 per cent, as the annual instalments paid by the beneficiaries to cover the purchase price of the land were substantially lower than the rents which were formerly paid.[9] Since then the instalments have been reduced and, instead of having to repay the full purchase price over 40 years, beneficiaries only pay 25 per cent of the expropriation costs. In Iraq the instalments remain higher, as beneficiaries have to meet 61 per cent of the purchase price over 40 years. The purchase price in Iran is arbitrarily fixed, being based on previous tax payments. Where landlords paid little tax, the purchase price was correspondingly low. However, the beneficiaries have to pay the full purchase price over 15 years, which is a difficult goal for many Iranian smallholders.[10]

The impact of land reform on the distribution of agricultural incomes is probably less than many reform protagonists believe, owing to the Muslim practice of dividing crops into 5 portions. This 'fiver' system means that shares of the agricultural produce not only go to those who own and work the land, but also to those who provide water for irrigation and seeds, as well as the suppliers of draught power for ploughing. Often the landlords themselves supply all these services, including the oxen for ploughing. Therefore reforms involving redistribution of land to the cultivators may only result in the latter's share of the produce rising by a fifth. Even where landlords are displaced as the customary suppliers of agricultural inputs, their functions are frequently taken over by unscrupulous middle men. In Egypt however, with the co-operatives supplying most necessary inputs, the cultivator's position is somewhat better. There, historically, this has also been the case as the government, rather than private sources, has always been responsible for providing irrigation water.

A redistribution of income from landlords to cultivators might be expected to result in a saving in foreign exchange, as luxury consumption, which often has a high import content, is reduced. There can be no doubt that the consumption levels of the former landlords were reduced to a considerable extent, especially as much of the compensation was never paid and the amounts fixed were below the market value of the land. Landlords were in any case forced to save as compensation took the form of bonds which were only redeemable after 30–40 years, except in Iran where cash was paid over a much shorter period.[11] The regulation of landlord–tenant relations and rent limitations, where effective, also probably adversely affected landlords incomes. Many landlords attempted to circumvent these reform measures, however, by various devious techniques. They exploited tenants who were in debt and often attempted to reassert their feudal positions.

The increase in living standards of the beneficiaries of land reform largely took the form of a rise in food consumption. This growth in food demand should have induced expansion in domestic agricultural production. Although farm production did increase by over 50 per cent during the period, however, as already stated, this hardly kept pace with the expansion in requirements due to population growth and could not cater for rising consumption levels. To some extent the food-pricing policies of the various governments were to blame, as these aimed at maintaining low food prices as far as possible, so that urban wages would be kept down in the interest of industrialisation.[12] The net effect of these cheap food policies, in conjunction with the land reforms, was to increase demand for food imports. Fortunately much of this demand was met through various food aid programmes and, in the case of Iraq and Iran, oil revenues could be used for food purchase. Nevertheless, most Middle Eastern governments do not wish to be dependent on food aid in the longer term, and the valuable foreign exchange earnings from oil could, it is felt, be more usefully deployed in acquiring essential imports necessary for development projects.

There is evidence that land reform has resulted in some adverse effects on employment.[13] On the redistributed plots usually only family labour will be employed. It has been estimated that in Egypt 5–10 per cent of the tenants and agricultural labourers working on the expropriated estates did not receive any land under the reform programme, and hence have joined the growing numbers of landless unemployed. Often these people were pushed out of the rural areas into the towns. Although no estimates have been made of the numbers adversely affected in this way in Iraq and Iran, it seems likely that the problem has arisen. Reference has already been made to the displacement of labour on the large mechanised holdings in Syria. Taking account of all these factors, it would appear that land reform has not proved a panacea for the Middle East's employment and food problems. Nor have the reforms achieved all their political objectives. Many of the former landlords have acquired urban real estate and are now influential city figures. Meanwhile in Syria and Iraq, the new military leaders now possess estates in the rural areas. Thus there remain many agrarian problems to be solved.

CO-OPERATIVES AND CREDIT FOR INVESTMENT IN AGRICULTURE

Throughout the Middle East, governments believe that co-operatives have an important role to play in rural development. The most far-reaching policy has been adopted in Syria, where land titles are vested in the co-operatives, which control all production and marketing operations. In Egypt and Iraq the co-operatives are responsible for provision of most inputs, credit facilities and marketing arrangements, while in addition they play an important part in the organisation of land use. Even in conservative Iran and Turkey, official encouragement is given to the co-operative movement, although their role in these countries has been limited mainly to credit provision.[14]

In Egypt the co-operatives set up following the land reform were designed to perform the functions previously undertaken by the landlords or their agents. These services included provision of seeds and fertilisers, as well as loans of bullocks or machinery for farm work. In addition it was hoped that the co-operatives could undertake marketing of agricultural produce, as well as providing storage and transport facilities, thus circumventing the middlemen who used to keep large margins for themselves. Control of farming operations on consolidated holdings was also placed in the hands of the co-operatives. In these tasks the Egyptian co-operatives were very successful throughout all the land reform areas, and this success led to an extension of the co-operative movement throughout the remaining farming areas of the Nile Valley, and the establishment of co-operative organisations with similar functions in Iraq.

It has already been observed that few economies of scale were achieved on the large estates expropriated during the Middle Eastern land reforms because, for operational purposes, they were subdivided amongst tenants and sharecroppers. Although smallholdings can produce high yields in the context of labour intensive agriculture, in Egypt some inefficiencies were readily apparent on these tiny plots. Much space was wasted with paths and boundaries, and deployment of equipment was difficult. Laying on irrigation facilities for each plot also presented problems. In addition, because in many cases cultivators had two or more separate fragments, often a considerable distance apart, time was wasted travelling between plots; while manuring of distant plots became a laborious task. The Muslim inheritance laws had undoubtedly accentuated this tendency towards subdivision. Naturally the Egyptian authorities feared that if ownership was subdivided to conform with these small operational units, which was in practice the substance of the land reform, a defective agrarian structure would be perpetuated, thus prejudicing future rural development prospects. The Egyptian Government decided that redistribution of land to the cultivators was necessary on political grounds, so that peasant aspirations would not be disappointed. However, at the same time as ownership was divided, it was proposed to enlarge the operational units through consolidation of fragmented holdings. Control of farming operations on these enlarged units would be placed in the hands of co-operatives, membership of which was made compulsory for all beneficiaries of the land reform. By adopting a dual agrarian structure of this type the authorities believed they could have the best of both worlds. The cultivators would have security of tenure through land ownership, while operational units would be large enough to overcome the disadvantages associated with fragmentation.

This scheme was a great success throughout those areas of Egypt which came within the scope of the land reform. Normally the co-operatives comprised around 400 hectares, and contained about 300 members each. Crops were consolidated into large blocks on the lands under the jurisdiction of each co-operative, and a triennial crop rotation was carried out. Crop yields increased remarkably on these consolidated blocks, owing in large measure to the intricate irrigation and drainage networks which were laid out and to the effective pest control implemented. Because of this success it was decided to extend the consolidation scheme throughout Egypt, to include those areas which did not come under the land reform. The control of land use was placed in the hands of the local co-operatives, which were being established throughout the country in any case, as mentioned earlier.[15]

When the Egyptian model of large operational units linked with peasant ownership was applied in Iraq, results were much less satisfactory. Although agricultural production has been increasing in Iraq, this has been largely due to an expansion of the area under cultivation, rather than through intensification of land use. Cotton and grain yields remain low, less than half Egyptian levels, and in many areas production remains below pre-land-reform levels. There seem to be several factors which can explain this apparent failure in applying the Egyptian model to Iraq.

(1) The co-operatives were beset with administrative problems owing to a lack of trained staff with the necessary organisational capabilities or agricultural knowledge.
(2) Before the land reform irrigation and drainage facilities had been

locally managed by landlords, or more frequently their agents. As there were few people in the co-operatives with the experience to run these facilities effectively, they fell into a state of disrepair in many areas. Soil salinity increased as drainage work was not undertaken. In Egypt, governmental authorities had always played a key role in the planning and maintenance of irrigation and drainage facilities, so delegation of some of these functions to the local co-operatives was a relatively simple matter.

(3)   Marketing of produce was a major problem for the co-operatives in Iraq. Unlike in Egypt, where well maintained feeder roads served most agricultural areas, the communications network in Iraq was poor and, during flooding, villages were often isolated for long periods. High transport costs had a disincentive effect, as payments to producers were correspondingly reduced.

(4)   The long delays in land redistribution during the reform programme discouraged cultivators, and caused much uncertainty throughout the rural areas. Naturally the former landlords were reluctant to play any part in the new co-operatives, yet these people retained strong local influence. Their opposition was undoubtedly an important factor which hindered development of the co-operative movement. As the former Egyptian landlords were often absentees, and in some cases foreigners, their links with the tenants and sharecroppers were remote. In Iraq, however, as many of the landlords were tribal sheiks, wielding vast feudal powers, their influence was not so easily destroyed.

In spite of the administrative difficulties encountered, the future role of co-operatives in the agricultural sectors of Iraq, Syria and Egypt seems assured. Continued government encouragement and financial support should help to ensure that the staffing position is improved, and that members' confidence will grow in their organisational stability over time. In Iran, however, the future of the co-operatives appears uncertain despite official lip-service in support of the movement. So far their role has been mainly limited to credit provision on a small scale, and attempts to provide ancillary services for the farming communities have met with little success. A few small retail shops have been set up to serve their members, but these have catered solely for household needs, and have not seriously challenged the traditional suppliers of agricultural inputs. The Iranian Government vacillated considerably over policy towards the co-operatives; placing the movement under the Ministry of Land Reform in 1967 was a severe blow. From then on, many of the members regarded the co-operative organisations as just another branch of a government machine they mistrusted.[16]

The traditional sources of agricultural credit throughout the Middle East was the private moneylenders. Frequently traders served in this capacity, providing seeds and other farm requisites on credit and collecting payments either in cash or in kind at harvest time. Loans were usually for small amounts and, although interest payments were high, the terms of the borrowing were flexible. It was this flexibility which made such credit popular with small farmers, as well as the absence of complicated application procedures, which meant loans could be negotiated speedily. Where credit was given in cash, moneylenders seldom worried about how the money was spent, as long as they received the interest payments and were eventually repaid. Naturally the risk of borrowers defaulting was great, and the high interest rates partly reflected this risk, although the relatively large administrative costs associated with small-scale lending were also responsible for these heavy servicing charges.

Landlords were another important source of credit in the Middle East. In fact traders who offered credit often became landowners, through borrowers failing to repay their debts, which resulted in land confiscation. After the land reforms, which meant the replacement of many landlords, it became necessary to set up alternative institutions to provide credit for small farmers. Although Agricultural Banks had been established in many Middle Eastern countries long before the land reforms, they were responsible for only a small portion of total credit granted, and their operations were directed at the larger farmers, rather than smallholders. As these banks were unsuitable for dealing directly with small landowners, it was decided in Egypt and Iran that the banks should lend to the co-operatives, which would be responsible for credit administration at the local level. In Iraq, funds are advanced to the co-operatives by a Co-operative Bank specially established for this type of activity, while in Syria a division of the General Federation of Co-operative Societies performs a similar function.[17]

Despite all these institutional innovations, the traditional moneylenders continue to play a dominant role in credit provision. To become a moneylender only modest capital is needed, which means even prosperous peasants can easily establish themselves in this type of business, as well as petty traders. Private moneylenders have a competitive advantage due to their local knowledge, which enables them to sort out the good from the bad risks. Local co-operative officials are often reluctant to offend any of the co-operative members through refusing loan applications. In addition, as these officials are only employees, and the money they are handling does not belong to them, there is a tendency to be careless in administering credit.

In an effort to avoid some of the problems associated with co-operative credit, the Egyptian authorities have established a 'Village Bank' project. By 1961 almost 150 branch banks had been opened in the rural areas under this scheme. Goods such as fertilisers, insecticides, etc. were advanced on a credit basis to individual co-operative members. Through this 'Village Bank' project it has been possible to mobilise rural savings which hitherto were hoarded, often in the form of gold. By encouraging farmers to bank their savings, these funds can be kept in circulation, and utilised to finance agricultural development. Given the large amount of hoarding throughout the Middle East, there seems considerable scope for modern financial institutions of this kind, so that the banking habit will be encouraged in other parts of the region.

EXTENSION OF IRRIGATION FACILITIES

Except for the coastal fringes of the Eastern Mediterranean, and the southern shores of the Black and Caspian Seas, most of the Middle East receives very little rainfall. Egyptian agriculture is concentrated in the Nile Valley and is totally dependent on irrigation while, although the northern parts of the Tigris–Euphrates Valley receive some winter rainfall, agriculture in Iraq and the Syrian interior is also largely based on irrigation. Rainfall reliability is as important as absolute amounts in the Middle East. The coastal regions of Syria, Lebanon and Israel are the only areas with dependable rainfall, this coming from November till March. Turkey and northwest and southwest Iran receive some winter rainfall also, but this is highly erratic, with considerable variations from year to year. Rain-fed agriculture is therefore a risky business in these areas, and hence dependence on irrigation is increased. In the Arabian Peninsula, which is largely desert, there is little agriculture, and the scope for irrigation is limited, except for a few oasis areas.

Irrigation in the Nile and Tigris–Euphrates Valley has a long history, extending back several thousand years. Some of the earliest recorded agricultural development occurred in these areas. More recently, under the guidance of Egypt's progressive ruler Muhammad Ali during the nineteenth century, a system of perennial irrigation was built up in the Nile Valley to cater for the cotton crop, which was introduced during this period.[18] This revolution laid the basis for Egypt's current system of agricultural production, which is heavily dependent on the cultivation of a single main cash crop—cotton—and based on labour intensive techniques, combined with a highly developed irrigation system.[19]

Irrigation by modern methods in the Tigris–Euphrates Valley only started in 1908 when the first barrage was constructed in Iraq. Since then, however, other schemes for flow irrigation through flood control have been instigated in both Iraq and Syria, although the irrigation network is not so extensive as in Egypt.

Salinisation has caused great problems in the Tigris–Euphrates Valley, because insufficient attention was paid to drainage works in the past. This resulted in the outright abandonment of land in some areas and meant that long periods of fallow for desalinisation were necessary in other places. Recently, more emphasis has been placed on drainage, especially in Iraq, a policy which should help intensify land use considerably. Investment in this sort of scheme should result in higher yields, and greater opportunities for labour absorption, emulating the Egyptian pattern. In cost–benefit terms this type of scheme is likely to give more favourable returns than the large farm mechanisation projects sponsored by the Syrian authorities. Drainage work requires a large input of unskilled labour, but little capital investment. Projects of this kind are therefore particularly suitable, given the current factor endowment of Syria and Egypt. The most viable type of mechanisation plans are small-scale ones, such as provision of pumping equipment to augment the irrigated areas. Such equipment is usually of simple design and could be produced locally rather than imported. This type of argument also applies to other kinds of irrigation equipment, such as tube-wells, which can be manufactured successfully in the rural districts where they are to be utilised, as the Pakistan experience shows.

These remarks on the merits of small-scale public works do not mean, however, that large schemes are necessarily precluded in the Middle East on the grounds of economic viability. Nevertheless, when assessing whether a large-scale project represents a sound investment, it is not enough to evaluate the scheme in terms of financial costs and benefits only. For example, at first sight the construction of the High Dam at Aswan appears to have been a worthwhile undertaking, as the benefits —a large increase in the cultivable area and additional electricity generation potential—seem substantial in relation to the expenditure involved.[20] On the negative side, however, some costs must be deducted from these returns. The floodwaters used to deposit silt along the valley, and this rejuvenated the agricultural land each year. As the Nile no longer floods, this silt merely accumulates behind the High Dam. Now farmers have to use fertilisers more intensively to maintain their former yields. In addition, salinisation has been a growing problem, and improved drainage works have proved necessary. Another drawback is the damage caused to the river banks below the dam due to the higher water flow sustained throughout the year. All these extra costs represent external diseconomies which have resulted from the Aswan scheme. Social costs have also been involved as the incidence of disease, especially bilharzia, has increased in the areas near the stagnant water behind the dam.[21] The investment criteria for large-scale irrigation projects should therefore incorporate all these factors. One means of doing this is by the use of shadow or accounting prices which allow for possible social costs. Even though such a method may make evaluation more difficult in quantitative cost terms, its use will at least ensure that planners become aware of the likely side-effects of any big scheme.

EXPORT VERSUS DOMESTIC PRODUCTION

A crucial dilemma facing Middle Eastern governments is whether to concentrate on production of industrial crops mainly destined for export markets, such as cotton, or alternatively to aim at increasing domestic production of food supplies to meet rising needs and save on agricultural imports.[22] In order to help employment creation it would be desirable to promote the expansion of both types of crop simultaneously. Unfortunately this is not possible, however, as the land available for cultivation in the Middle East only represents a small proportion of the total area, varying from under 3 per cent in Egypt to slightly below one-third in Syria, Lebanon and Turkey, where there is most arable land. Even with an extension of irrigation, and further intensification of land use, it seems likely that land will remain the main limiting factor of production.[23] This means there is an opportunity cost in industrial crop cultivation, in terms of lost food production, and vice versa in the case of food crops. Given this trade-off situation between industrial and food crops, economic theory would suggest that each country should specialise in those lines of agricultural production in which they have a comparative advantage. As the net value added per hectare for cotton is almost three times that for any grain crop, this would seem to indicate that the Middle Eastern countries should concentrate on this type of industrial crop, and use their export earnings to purchase food requirements from countries which have a comparative advantage in the latter.

Increased specialisation in industrial crops such as textile fibres, is hindered by difficult market prospects. Middle Eastern cotton, for example, faces increasing competition from synthetic fibres, and during the last 20 years other countries outside the region, especially the Soviet

Union, have increased their cotton production considerably. In addition the United States has pursued disruptive export policies as a consequence of the overproduction problems facing its Southern states. These worldwide trends have resulted in adverse price effects for Middle Eastern producers, causing considerable instability of export earnings.[24] In Egypt the four ways of overcoming these external market difficulties have been through area restrictions, export taxes, buffer stock policies, and subsidies and exchange rate adjustments. There may seem to be a contradiction in applying export taxes and subsidies at the same time. However, in practice, given the imperfect markets in which Egypt has to deal, subsidies have been used for certain export deals, while export taxes have been more uniform. The subsidies are a means of adjusting prices to suit conditions in each particular market.

Given these marketing difficulties with industrial crops, it may seem more appropriate for the Middle Eastern governments to aim at domestic self-sufficiency in food production, hence saving foreign exchange which can be used instead for capital imports to promote industrialisation. In this type of policy, however, the Middle Eastern countries face several disadvantages, the principal one being, as already mentioned, the lower value added per hectare in grain production. In addition, as cultivation of grain crops is less labour intensive than that of textile fibres, such a production policy would merely worsen the employment situation. Any horizontal expansion of food crops in Egypt's irrigated areas would mean that the tri-annual rotational system would have to be abandoned. Yet this system has proved extremely effective in soil conservation, and its replacement by a biennial rotation may only result in declining yields. In the Nile Valley a complementarity between grain and industrial crops exists at present; to regard them as substitutes may be misleading, beyond a certain point, given the rotational restraints.

Nevertheless, despite the limited prospects for horizontal expansion of either grain or industrial crops, owing to the relatively fixed land area and the complementarities in production just discussed, there remains considerable scope for vertical expansion through intensification of production. Given the limited resources at the policy maker's disposal, however, he will still have to decide to concentrate his efforts. As with the horizontal expansion considered earlier, vertical expansion of grain cultivation may have an opportunity cost in terms of lost production of industrial crops. Where new inputs and extension services are directed towards intensifying one type of production, other lines may stagnate or actually decline.

Crop yields vary considerably in the Middle East, output per hectare being highest in the Nile Valley, and lowest in the Tigris–Euphrates Valley, while the northern tier countries, Iran and Turkey, occupy an intermediate position. Although the Egyptian yields compare favourably with most other parts of the Middle East, in a worldwide comparison the yields obtained do not appear to be particularly outstanding. In cotton for example, a crop especially suited to the factor environment of the Nile Valley, the Soviet Union has now surpassed Egypt, with yields over 30 per cent higher.[25] Observers often point to the high Egyptian grain yields in comparison to the Soviet Union or United States as evidence of the achievements made by Nile Valley farmers. However, it is misleading to compare the labour intensive cultivation of grain in Egypt with the extensive mechanised farming of these large continental sized super powers. Egyptian grain yields are about average for the Mediterranean area, which represents a more meaningful comparison, but they remain well below the yields attained in northwest Europe.

The higher crop yields obtained in Egypt compared to elsewhere in the Middle East can be attributed to the widespread use of fertiliser in the Nile Valley. At present, however, the scope for further fertiliser application in Egypt is limited, unless there are substantial cost reductions, because the marginal returns in terms of additional output have been declining sharply in recent years. Fortunately, most other areas in the Middle East are far from reaching this stage. In the Tigris–Euphrates Valley for example, virtually no fertilisers were used before 1960, and efforts to promote their use since then have met with only modest success. The relatively poor agricultural performance of Iraq and Syria reflects to a large extent their minimal use of fertiliser, which is under one-tenth of Egyptian levels. Of the two northern tier countries, fertilisers use is more widespread in Turkey than Iran. The potential gains from increased use of nitrogenous and phosphate fertilisers should prove especially large in Iran, given the continuing low yields there, which are not far above the 1950 levels in grain production.

Recently, new high-yielding dwarf varieties of wheat and hybrid maize have been introduced into the Middle East, and these may result in a 'Green Revolution'[26] of comparable dimensions to that which has occurred in southeast Asia.[27] These 'miracle' seeds have caused dramatic increases in agricultural output in many other parts of the Third World. Their introduction into the Middle East may ultimately result in countries becoming self-sufficient in food production throughout the area. Unlike southeast Asia this can have few adverse effects on intra-regional trade in agricultural commodities, as this is minimal in any case in the Middle East. An encouraging feature of these seed innovations is their neutrality with regard to scale in production, and consequent consistency with the existing systems of small-scale agriculture found throughout the Middle East. In addition, the effects on employment in these labour surplus economies are likely to be favourable. The intensification of production should directly increase demands for labour in agriculture, while the additional farm incomes generated may have multiplier effects on employment in the manufacturing and service sectors.

One danger resulting from this type of seed innovation is that the subsequent increased production will lead to lower farm produce prices. This could reduce incentives for producers and have adverse effects on employment in agriculture. The effects on other sectors of the economy may be more favourable, however. Lower food prices might keep down industrial wages, thus helping to maintain low costs in manufacturing. These lower costs could in turn induce further industrial expansion and hence generate additional employment opportunities. In addition, consumption may be stimulated, even where industrial wages remain static, as industrial worker's real disposable incomes increase because of lower food prices. This may also have a favourable multiplier effect on domestic employment, assuming that little of this extra expenditure is on imports, income 'leakages' abroad being minimal.

It is difficult to determine how producers have responded to agricultural price changes in the Middle East from the experience of the last 20 years.[28] The main problem is to separate price effects from the consequences of other government policies. From the scanty evidence available it seems probable that the net effect of government intervention in commodity markets has been negative as far as producers are concerned, and may have acted as a disincentive to produce. With food supply failing to keep pace with the growth in total demand from an increasing population, food prices have risen considerably in the Middle East during the period under review. However, the rises have not been as great as they might have been under freer market conditions. It appears that the internal terms of trade have turned against agriculture, except in the northern tier countries where Government intervention in commodity markets has been limited to stabilisation.

The Arab governments have maintained price control policies which have aimed not merely at stabilisation, but also at affecting the underlying trend by containing upward price movements. These policies, which date from the Second World War period, are in the interests of consumers rather than producers. They may help industrialisation, but from the point of view of agricultural producers the policies are scarcely encouraging. Although the transformation of traditional agriculture is primarily a techno-organisational problem, and direct cropping area controls can play an important part in determining production as in Egypt, price incentives do affect intensification through their impact on certain key variables such as the profitability of fertiliser application, as already mentioned. In the Middle East, much of agricultural production is for consumption by the producer, but government pricing policies can affect this proportion. Higher prices mean a larger surplus will be available to meet urban needs, while farmers offered lower prices will market less of their crop. Therefore, paradoxically, price controls designed in the interests of industrialisation may have the effect of reducing food supplies to urban areas, as farm families consume more of their own production.[29]

To many development theorists the debate about whether to promote industry or agriculture appears rather sterile, as both sectors are believed to be interdependent. It is argued that increasing incomes in rural areas enhance the market prospects for manufactured products, while an expanded urban market provides a useful outlet for agricultural products. Unfortunately, in the Middle East such favourable intra-sectoral linkages have not been established to any significant extent. In spite of the redistribution effected through land reforms, rural incomes remain low owing to rapid population increase. As few cultivators have even modest amounts of disposable income remaining after meeting their families' food requirements, their demand for manufactured goods is minimal. Meanwhile, increasing urban food requirements have been met largely through imports under aid programmes such as the U.S. PL 480 scheme, rather than from domestic sources. The favourable linkages have been limited to a handful of industries. Increasing rural demand for chemical fertiliser has led to the establishment of modern plants for its manufacture; but these employ few people. An increasing demand for cloth resulted in the setting up of new textile factories, which provide a useful outlet for locally produced cotton. In Egypt, cotton producers have benefited little from this, however, as government policy has aimed at keeping down cotton prices, so that input costs are minimised for the textile factories to keep them competitive. Israel is the only country where there has been a substantial creation of agro-industries bringing benefits to agricultural producers, factory employees and consumers. These industries have been mainly concerned with the canning and processing of citrus fruit for export. There is considerable scope for diversification into this kind of production elsewhere in the Middle East.

Although in the short term it may be difficult to compete in European markets with the established citrus fruit exporters in quality of produce, it should be possible to undercut in price as Morocco has already done.

Expansion of beef production not only could prove profitable for producers, but may also have favourable linkages with the industrial sector. At present, livestock production represents 40–50 per cent of value added in Middle Eastern agriculture. Much of the rain-fed land which is unsuitable for cultivation can be used for grazing. Yet mutton and lamb production has remained virtually stagnant during the last decade in Turkey, Iran, Syria and Iraq, while beef production has done little better. Average carcass weights remain low, because little effort is made to improve the quality of stock. The current emphasis on quantity rather than quality is largely due to animals being regarded by most farmers as a source of traction power, and not merely looked at in terms of meat production. Control of stock numbers seems to be essential if the problems of overgrazing are to be overcome.[30] In addition, efforts should be made to improve the quality of stock, through increasing application of artificial insemination. At present, improved breeds account for less than 5 per cent of livestock in the Middle East. More effective disease-control programmes will have to be undertaken, however, to reduce the risks involved in investing in grade stock. Increased output of forage crops can also help meat production, because carcass weights are improved. Egyptian farmers have achieved some success in this respect. Investment in livestock improvement is likely to give high returns, as the increasing consumption throughout the Middle East means an assured market. At present, a growing proportion of this market is being supplied through imports, so increasing domestic production should help to save foreign exchange.

Agriculture still represents the major employer of labour in the Middle East, with between a half and three-quarters of the economically active population engaged in agriculture in most of the area. Governments throughout the Middle East tend to see development in terms of increasing industrial employment, largely at the expense of agriculture. However, the trends of the past 20 years show that although the share of industry in national product has steadily risen, the increase in industrial employment is much slower. Absolute numbers employed in agriculture continue to increase, though only slowly, and it seems that this trend is not likely to change in the foreseeable future, since the employment opportunities generated in other sectors are insufficient to absorb the growing available workforce. The question arises whether an increase in numbers in the agricultural sector will lead merely to underemployment or to even greater open unemployment in the rural areas if it proves impossible to employ the additional labour.

In the past, it appears, much of the unemployment problem in Middle Eastern agriculture has been seasonal, though a small amount of open unemployment has existed even during periods of peak labour requirements. At first glance there seems to be no underemployment, with the evidence suggesting that labours' marginal productivity is positive, as workforce reductions lead to falls in agricultural output.[31] This evidence relates to large farms; on the majority of small farms there is probably a considerable amount of disguised unemployment, caused by geographical immobility and the traditional rigid work demarcation between different categories of labour. Thus underemployment is accentuated to a large extent by institutional factors such as the land tenure system. The land distribution programmes may have worsened this situation. Nevertheless, if the growth of labour supply continues to outpace the growth of employment opportunities outside agriculture, then underemployment of this type may be preferable on social and political grounds to open unemployment in urban areas. The cost of not absorbing this surplus labour in agriculture could be very high when measured in terms of social unrest and political instability. In retrospect therefore the promotion of labour intensive methods of farming may seem the most appropriate policy to have adopted, given the relative rates of productive factor growth experienced in the Middle East.

TRADE PROSPECTS FOR AGRICULTURAL PRODUCE

Given the limited scope for horizontal expansion of agricultural production, and the difficulty of promoting investment in the rural areas because of the continuing land tenure problems as well as the lack of effective credit institutions, the prospects for expanding exports of agricultural produce seem severely limited for most Middle Eastern countries. None of the Arab countries have built up marketing organisations comparable to those established in Israel. Only a small proportion of Egyptian citrus produce finds its way to outside markets, and these are largely confined to eastern Europe.[32] In contrast, the Israeli marketing organisation goes to considerable lengths to promote Jaffa produce throughout western Europe, and even undertakes costly, but rewarding, advertising campaigns in the West. At present, their main campaign is

designed to encourage Western housewives to purchase more grapefruit.
All Jaffa produce are strictly graded and carefully packed, whereas
elsewhere in the Middle East citrus fruit is seldom graded.

One of the major problems facing Middle Eastern agricultural producers is overdependence on a single crop. This makes producers
extremely vulnerable to price fluctuation, or even continuous declines.
Table 2.2 illustrates how five of the main agricultural exporters of the

TABLE 2.2. Main agricultural export as a proportion of total exports

Country	Main merchandise export	Period	% of total merchandise exports
Egypt	Raw cotton	av. 1972–73	47·2
Lebanon	Fruit and vegetables	av. 1969–71	14·0
Sudan	Raw cotton	av. 1969–71	60·9
Syria	Raw cotton	av. 1969–71	40·9
North Yemen	Coffee	av. 1969–71	38·0
South Yemen	Raw cotton	av. 1968–71	46·5

Note: All figures are the latest reliable estimate available.
Source: Kuwait Fund for Arab Economic Development, *The Arab World:
    Key Indicators*, Kuwait, April 1975.

Middle East are dependent on a single crop for well over a third of their
total export earnings; while in the case of Sudan this dependence is over
60 per cent. There has been some tendency for the proportion of export
earnings generated by one product to decline in recent years, but it is
interesting to note that even in Egypt, despite the country's ambitious
industrialisation programmes, raw cotton still accounts for almost half
of total export earnings.[33] In South Yemen and Syria the proportion of
raw cotton exports to total exports is almost as high as in Egypt, although the actual volume of exports is of course much lower than ship-
ments out of Alexandria. Like Egypt, Syria is, however, increasingly
exporting cotton textiles rather than raw cotton, which means the value
added in production accrues to the local economy, rather than to the
economy of the developed country where the produce is marketed.

Two of the countries cited in the table, Lebanon and North Yemen,
market a large portion of their main export product within the Middle
East. Lebanese fruit and vegetables are marketed extensively in the Gulf

area after being sent overland by truck, while the country's apples are sold throughout the Arab world.[34] Similarly, coffee from North Yemen has acquired a reputation in many Arab countries for its excellent taste and consequently tends to dominate the local market, often commanding a premium price over other blends.[35] It is interesting to note that both Lebanon and North Yemen improved their terms of trade during the early 1970s, largely because of the buoyant market within the Middle East for their main agricultural exports. In contrast, those countries dependent on world cotton markets fared badly. Egypt's net barter terms of trade declined by over 11 per cent between 1968 and 1970 alone. This was largely due to the adverse conditions prevailing in the market for long staple cotton. Although Sudan, which produces cheaper grade cotton, fared slightly better, it did experience a 5 per cent decline in its terms of trade during the 1968–70 period. Both Egypt and Sudan were successful in expanding their exports of other non-agricultural items over this period to compensate for the decline in the value of cotton exports; so, in terms of purchasing power, the two countries ended up better-off than before, despite the adverse terms of trade. Nevertheless, this improvement only amounted to around 4 per cent per annum for each country, which was insufficient to alleviate the severe foreign exchange shortages experienced by the two states.[36]

The major agricultural producing nations of the Middle East would clearly have been ill-advised to continue their dependence on one export line over whose price they had little control. Even if the adverse terms of trade of recent years were reversed for crops such as cotton, there was no guarantee that any improvements made could be sustained. Fluctuations in export prices can have almost as detrimental an effect on a country's development as the adverse price trends first postulated by Prebisch over 20 years ago. A country may suddenly find itself short of the foreign exchange it needs to purchase necessary capital imports, as was the case in Egypt in the 1960s. Long-term planning in these circumstances may prove impossible, because new projects may often have to be delayed, or even abandoned, owing to foreign exchange constraints. Under such conditions, specialisation in agricultural commodities for export according to the principle of comparative advantage appeared to lead up a developmental cul-de-sac as far as the economies of the Middle East were concerned. Governments in the area increasingly recognised this in the 1950s as, with growing nationalistic feelings, the value of the established trading arrangements started to be questioned. There was an increasing emphasis on economic self-reliance and a desire to lessen the dependence on a few primary commodities; but this could only be achieved through economic diversification. In order to break out of the old economic order, free trade policies were gradually abandoned, and governments instead decided to encourage import substitution behind tariffs. These policies will be examined in the next chapter.

3 Import Substitution

In recent years most of the countries of the Middle East have become increasingly aware of the difficulties associated with relying on export trade as the main 'engine of growth'. The pricing and production limitations faced by the leading agricultural producers in the area have just been discussed in the previous chapter. Even in the oil-producing states, however, there is a growing realisation that overdependence on the export of one commodity makes them extremely vulnerable to changes in world market conditions. It is true of course that the oil-producing nations have been successful in organising themselves into a cartel to control supplies through OPEC in a way that no group of agricultural producers has been able to emulate.[1] Without the political will to agree amongst the Arab members that the October 1973 war and its aftermath provided, it seems unlikely that OPEC would have been so successful in raising the price of oil. Throughout the decade before this war, the price of oil had been falling in real terms, and the terms of trade of the major producing nations had been deteriorating. Since the price rises of 1974 this downward trend is again apparent, as the limited price rises agreed in September 1975 have not compensated the OPEC producers for the increased prices that they have to pay for imports of industrial goods from the West.

Vulnerability to adverse price trends, and uncertainty with regard to fluctuations in market prices for primary commodities, provides an economic rationale for the adoption of an import substitution policy as an alternative to specialisation in export production. It is difficult for countries to plan ahead when it is impossible to assess what foreign exchange will be available to finance the purchase even of items such as food imports. In addition, it is politically degrading for Third World countries to have to go cap-in-hand and virtually beg for foreign exchange credits to tide them over the balance of payments difficulties which low export prices bring. Yet the Arab world's richest oil state, Saudi Arabia, had to do this in the early 1960s, although admittedly this was a result of King Saud's lavish expenditure at the time, rather than because of any pressing need on the part of his subjects for imported goods.[2] Countries dependent on one export market are in a particularly vulnerable position, as was the case in Egyptian–Soviet trade, or the Gulf trade with Britain until the late 1960s, or the trade of the Magreb nations with France before and after independence. Yet even when countries go to a multinational agency for assistance, such as the World Bank, or International Monetary Fund, they may resent its interference in their economic affairs, since such agencies usually sent out their own 'experts' to assist countries which they have aided.

The main motivation for the adoption of import substitution policies in the Middle East has undoubtedly been political rather than economic, and these policies are perhaps best viewed as an economic manifestation of the desire for national independence, as well as being part of the nation-building process. Governments in the Middle East tend to see economic diversification as an integral part of this process and want to modernise their economies as the nations of both the Western and Communist world have done. Every country in the area, irrespective of its political ideology, wants to industrialise, as this is regarded as the only real way to develop, and the agrarian sector, even where it makes the main contribution to economic activity and exports, is usually seen as backward. Agricultural progress is considered a totally unsuitable means of economic transformation, and an industrial revolution is thought of as a necessary prerequisite regardless of local conditions. Arab socialists, in particular, wanted to see industrial employment expanded as this would result in the emergence of an urban proletariat who normally provide the grassroots support for leftist parties.[3] Rural peasants in contrast, in the Middle East as elsewhere, tend to be conservative. The desire for modernisation in the region is such, however, that even conservative political regimes, such as those in Iran, Saudi Arabia or Jordan, are encouraging rapid industrialisation through import substitution in spite of the political risks involved.

MOVES TOWARDS ECONOMIC DIVERSIFICATION

Although virtually all the countries of the Middle East have now adopted import substitution policies, the degree of progress varies considerably, as does the range of commodities for which local manufacturing plants have been established or planned. Iran was the first country in the region to set up infant industries behind tariffs back in the 1930s, and the policy has now been in operation so long that some of the early industries established must be considered as mature. Most of the investment in these early years was in petroleum because, despite the fact that by 1930 Iran was a major oil producer, virtually all the country's own oil consumption needs were met by supplies from the Soviet Union. There was no local refining capacity, and Iran exported its crude oil, and imported refined products.[4] The same trade situation prevailed in the major Arab oil-producing nations until the 1950s, when the first refining capacity was established in the Arabian peninsula, but even today the oil-rich states still have to import many petroleum-based products which their own, relatively unsophisticated refinery plants cannot produce. Local multiplier effects from establishing refineries to produce import substitutes are in any case minimal, as this type of industry is by nature highly capital intensive and creates few employment opportunities. A large proportion of the more highly skilled workforce who man these plants are expatriates, who remit a substantial part of their salaries to their home countries, while their local consumption is usually met from imported goods.

Of the non-oil-exporting states, Egypt and Turkey have progressed furthest with import substitution policies, as Table 3.1 indicates. Virtually all of the import substitution has been in the field of manufacturing industry, so its share of gross domestic product serves as a good indicator of progress with such policies. Manufacturing industry accounts for over 17 per cent of gross domestic product in Egypt, while the share of agriculture has declined to below one-third.[5] Egypt has developed the most highly diversified economy in the Arab world, about which more will be said presently in a separate section in this chapter. The share of manufacturing industry in Turkey is even higher, and now amounts to almost one-quarter of G.D.P., while agriculture's share has been reduced so far that it is only slightly greater than this. Turkey, like Egypt, has a large market despite its low per capita income, and the cash economy has spread to take in the entire population of the country including those living in the most remote areas. Both countries have large urban centres, with a labour force accustomed to working the long regular hours associated with the early stages of most industrial revolutions in the past. Turkey has an additional advantage as large numbers of its workers have gained industrial experience through being employed as migrant labourers in West Germany and elsewhere in Europe, and these people are therefore accustomed to modern manufacturing plants.[6] During the recent recession in Europe, many of the semi-skilled, and even some of the skilled, workers returned to Turkey. Often

TABLE 3.1. Gross domestic product by economic sector (percentage)

Country	Year	Agri-culture	Extractive industry	Manufac-turing industry	Construc-tion	Trade	Trans-port	Other
Egypt	1973	29·0	0·9	17·4	2·9	8·5	4·3	36·7
Iran	1973	11·6	41·2	11·4	4·2	5·5	3·1	23·1
Iraq	1971	12·7	34·9	10·4	2·9	7·0	5·4	26·7
Israel	1973	4·8	——20·5——		9·8	8·6	6·9	49·2
Jordan	1974	18·3	——15·3——		6·3	17·3	8·1	33·7
Kuwait	1973	0·2	68·6	5·6	1·0	5·3	3·1	16·2
Lebanon	1972	9·9	——15·9——		4·6	31·5	7·5	30·6
Libya	1972	2·6	57·5	2·2	7·9	3·8	4·5	21·4
Saudi Arabia	1972	2·8	65·0	6·8	4·5	3·8	5·2	11·9
Sudan	1971	32·4	0·4	12·4	3·5	18·7	6·8	25·7
Syria	1974	21·0	9·7	14·2	4·8	20·9	6·9	22·6
Tunisia	1974	18·3	10·7	10·3	6·8	14·8	4·7	34·4
Turkey	1974	28·1	1·4	24·5	5·0	12·6	8·0	20·4
Yemen	1973	61·4	0·7	2·6	3·9	14·5	2·4	14·4
D. Yemen	1970	19·4	0·0	26·9	0·7	12·7	5·4	35·0

Source: *U.N. Statistical Yearbook*, 1974.

these workers are prepared even during boom conditions to accept wages in Turkey which are only a small portion of those they could earn elsewhere, as they prefer to work in their own country.

The other main country in the Middle East with a major manufacturing sector is Israel and, in terms of the sectoral shares of G.D.P., it corresponds to the industrial states of Europe, rather than to the developing economies of its neighbours. Despite the importance of the agricultural sector's contribution to export earnings, its share of gross domestic production is below 5 per cent. Industrial activity, in contrast, most of which is in manufacturing, accounts for over one-fifth of gross domestic product, and most of this is consumed locally while competing imports are excluded from the market. A wide range of consumer goods, including durables, are manufactured, and the country's range of domestically produced intermediate products is increasing, although many of these are exported because of the limited size of the home market.[7]

From Table 3.1 it would appear that South Yemen (formerly Aden) has more manufacturing proportionally than any other country in the Middle East. This is largely a legacy of the days of British rule, as there were many small establishments at that time catering largely for the servicemen's needs. Since British withdrawal there has been little development in the country, and the large proportion of G.D.P. accounted for by the manufacturing sector only reflects the underdevelopment of the rest of the economy. This is not the case, however, in Jordan, Lebanon or Syria, all of which have growing manufacturing sectors, although manufacturing activity accounts for less than one-seventh of total economic activity in each of these countries.[8] Much of the industry based in Lebanon consists of light, consumer-orientated manufacturing plants, while in Syria, in contrast, there is more heavy industry, although this is also geared to the requirements of the domestic market.

Despite the efforts being made to promote manufacturing activity in the oil-rich states of the region, none of these economies, apart from Iran's, can boast a large manufacturing sector. Even in Iran the proportion of gross domestic product accounted for by manufacturing is below one-eighth, but it must be admitted that comparisons with non-oil states can be misleading in this instance, owing to the size and absolute importance of the petroleum sector in the Iranian economy. To some extent the same applies to Iran's neighbour, Iraq, although there political instability has until recently meant a lack of continuity in plans for industrial development.

In the other oil-exporting states, manufacturing industry outside the oil sector has only been established during the last decade, and in spite

TABLE 3.2. Increase in output by economic sector (percentage)

Country	Year	Agri-culture	Total industry	Manufac-turing industry	Construc-tion	Trade	Trans-port	Other
Egypt	1960–70	4·7	6·0	—	11·4	4·0	−1·9	7·0
	1970–71	4·0	3·2	—	1·8	6·6	2·4	5·4
Iran	1960–70	1·4	13·6	—	8·5	8·7	4·4	11·5
	1970–72	2·0	14·8	—	13·2	10·5	9·7	19·9
Libya	1962–70	2·3	33·0	10·4	19·4	13·3	19·0	14·1
	1970–71	16·3	−17·1	7·8	3·1	27·5	44·7	5·7
Saudi Arabia	1962–70	1·4	11·7	11·2	6·9	10·2	14·3	8·0
	1970–71	3·2	21·1	0·4	10·0	9·0	5·2	6·3
Syria	1960–70	4·4	6·8	5·6	3·7	4·3	6·6	7·5
	1970–73	1·3	8·2	6·7	6·4	4·0	11·2	11·2
Tunisia	1961–70	0·5	11·4	7·6	3·5	4·1	8·0	3·5
Turkey	1970–73	16·3	11·8	17·1	10·5	15·4	4·1	5·2
	1960–70	2·5	10·3	10·8	7·3	8·7	8·6	4·9
Yemen	1970–73	0·2	11·8	12·5	4·4	12·1	8·0	—
	1969–70	0·9	6·7	7·2	0·0	17·2	3·2	1·5

Source: *U.N. Statistical Yearbook*, 1974.

of their ambitious plans for industrialisation, the projects contemplated are still at a very early stage. Saudi Arabia and Kuwait have a much wider range of industry than Libya, where manufacturing contributes a mere 2·2 per cent of gross domestic product. A large proportion of government funds for industrialisation in Saudi Arabia have been devoted to the construction of a large steel mill which is not yet fully operational. Despite the vast financial resources of these countries, however, prospects for rapid industrialisation do not appear promising, given the manpower shortages, the limited extent of local markets, and the difficulty infant industries set up in such unfavourable environments would have competing in international markets.

The increase in output by economic sector for eight of the main countries in the Middle East is illustrated in Table 3.2. Unfortunately, the range of countries is restricted owing to the lack of data for the time period covered in many of the smaller countries which have only recently improved their statistical services. The table shows that, although the rises in industrial output have been impressive in most of the countries cited, other sectors have also been expanding rapidly, despite the fact that they have not had the same financial resources at their disposal, or as great an encouragement from the governments concerned. In Egypt, for example, during the 1960s the construction sector was expanding almost twice as rapidly as industrial activity, most of which was accounted for by manufacturing. The main reason for this building boom was that the construction sector was excluded from the nationalisation which applied to most industry and represented one of the few fields of economic activity in which private investors could participate. In the early 1970s commerce was the fastest-growing sector in Egypt, partly as a consequence of the opening up of the economy under Sadat to Western and Arab investors, but also because of the expansion of internal trading activity as the economy picked up again following the post-1967 recession.[9]

In Iran, as in Egypt, data is only available for the total increase in industrial output, and a separate breakdown is not given for manufacturing. To a large extent the rapid expansion in output is accounted for by the petroleum sector, and the increase in manufacturing production is probably much less impressive. It is interesting to note the poor performance of the agricultural sector, in spite of the land reform, and the ambitious co-operative programme. The rate of agricultural expansion has steadily fallen, and it remains the Achilles' heel of the Iranian economy. In neighbouring Turkey the record of the agricultural sector has been even less impressive, with production virtually stagnant in the

1970s. Most of the economic growth in Turkey has been accounted for by the manufacturing sector, which produces mainly import substitutes for the domestic market.[10] The rate of growth of manufacturing output increased in the 1970s to over 12 per cent per annum as the table shows, the best performance of all the countries cited, except for Tunisia, which has only a small industrial base in any case. Apart from Iran, Egypt and Turkey, Syria is the only other country included which has an established industrial base. There, as in Egypt, the increase in manufacturing output would undoubtedly have been greater had it not been for the open conflicts with Israel and the diversion of resources into military activities. A substantial part of Syria's industrial capacity was actually destroyed in the 1973 conflict, when the country's main oil refinery and steel plant were directly bombarded.

The most surprising figures presented in Table 3.2 are undoubtedly those for Saudi Arabia, where industrial progress was far from impressive in the 1960s given the country's almost negligible manufacturing base at the start of the period, which makes the attainment of a high growth rate relatively easy.[11] In the early 1970s, manufacturing output was in fact nearly stagnant as the table shows, in spite of the country's vast financial resources and the government's desire to encourage industrialisation. At the same time, however, Saudi Arabia's construction sector expanded at a much higher rate than in the 1960s, using scarce labour resources which could instead have been engaged in manufacturing activity. Some of this construction involved basic infrastructure, which is admittedly a prerequisite for industrialisation, but much of it was of residential housing, hospitals, schools and military installations, which make no direct contribution to economic growth despite their social desirability. Libya, which has a similar economic structure to Saudi Arabia, developed, perhaps not surprisingly, in almost the same way during the 1960s. In Libya, trade and commerce was one of the most rapidly expanding sectors, but most of the trade was in imported goods, as the country produces few domestic substitutes. Recently the Libyan government has sought to expand domestic agricultural production to attain a measure of economic independence through cutting down food imports.[12] This policy has met with some success in terms of increased output as the table indicates, although this has only been achieved at enormous financial cost. Given the size of Libya's oil revenue in relation to the country's population, such costs are not a problem, in spite of the fall in oil production in the early 1970s, which accounts for the contraction in industrial output indicated in the table, and more recent similar contractions. In a country such as Libya, oil conservation may be the best means of safeguarding the future, as the prospects for import substitution are poor because of the restricted local market and the shortage of labour or any other resources apart from petroleum.

PROMOTION OF INDUSTRY IN EGYPT

In contrast to Libya, Egypt has the advantage of a large workforce, many members of which have some education or training, and a well established domestic market, even though the per capita income is only £120 sterling. It is interesting therefore to consider Egypt as a case study of import substitution in the Middle East, especially as this country has a longer experience of implementing this type of policy than any other Arab country, and so highlights some of the problems which the other states may be expected to face.[13] It makes an interesting contrast with Iran, the other country chosen for detailed analysis in this chapter, as it is not a major oil exporter.

The last 20 years in Egypt have witnessed what amounts to an industrial revolution. There has been a tremendous expansion in output in all the major industrial sectors as Table 3.3 shows.[14] The expansion has been particularly marked in the chemical, pharmaceutical, engineering and electrical industries. Within these industries there has been an expansion at all stages of production. Thus in the chemical industry there has been an increase not only in production of consumer goods such as soap and detergents, but also of agricultural inputs such as fertiliser. The latter can be looked upon as a capital goods industry. In the metal industry, production of steel has expanded steadily at Helwan, and this steel is used for production of consumer durables for the domestic market, including car bodies, air conditioners, refrigerators, washing machines, sewing machines, bicycles, etc. Electricity for much of this industrial activity comes from the High Dam at Aswan. Egypt thus has a solid industrial base with many inter-sectoral and inter-industry linkages. The emergences of such linkages helps account for the geographical concentration of Egyptian manufacturing in the major cities of the lower Nile Valley and Delta.[15] The electronics industry in the Cairo and Alexandria urban regions enjoys major external economies as a result of location. The television and radio manufacturers are able to obtain locally produced tubes, valves, wires, cables and batteries where necessary.

The majority of Egypt's industries, even at the consumer goods level,

TABLE 3.3. Value of industrial output

Sector	'000 L.E. at current prices				% value by sector 1952	% value by sector 1969	% increase in output 1952–71	% increase in output 1966–71
	1952	1966	1969	1971				
Petroleum industries	34·2	103·2	110·2	152·2	11	7	345	47
Mining	3·6	12·1	10·8	N/A	1	1	200	−11
Chemicals and pharmaceuticals	20·5	142·2	164·1	155·9	6	11	660	10
Food industries	122·3	308·7	425·2	485·6	39	28	297	57
Engineering and electrical industries	30·1	155·6	233·2	235·6	10	15	683	51
Building material industries	8·4	34·6	44·5	59·7	3	3	611	73
Spinning and weaving industries	84·6	383·4	449·9	510·9	27	30	504	33
Electric energy	10·6	48·4	73·2	N/A	3	5	590	51
Total	313·8	1188·2	1511·1	N/A	100	100	382	27

Notes: The total percentage increases in output (bottom line) and the increases for mining and electric energy run up to 1969 only. These increases would be much less impressive if they were quoted in terms of constant prices. Figures on inflation rates are not available, however, for particular industrial sectors.

Source: Central Agency for Public Mobilisation and Statistics, *Statistical Handbook*, June 1972.

are in the state sector. This state participation resulted from pragmatic considerations rather than through ideological motivation, as will be shown.[16] In the early years of this century Egypt concentrated at first on establishment of industries in which it had a comparative advantage, given its factor endowment. With the existing pattern of agricultural production, and local food and clothing demands, it was not surprising then that the first industries established were associated with food processing and cotton textiles. Cotton ginning, pressing, spinning and weaving were all established before the First World War. Even at that time, over one-tenth of Egypt's labour force was engaged in industry as Table 3.4 shows. Industrial production was expanded somewhat in the

TABLE 3.4. Distribution of the labour force by sector (percentage)

Sector	1907	1917	1927	1937	1947	1960	1970
Agriculture	70·5	68·5	67·0	69·0	62·4	58·0	48·9
Industry	11·0	11·5	10·6	10·6	12·3	12·6	16·0
Commerce and transportation	7·6	10·0	12·5	10·4	12·1	11·7	13·9
Services	10·9	10·0	9·9	10·0	13·2	17·7	21·2

Sources: 1907–1960: Egyptian Central Agency for Public Mobilisation and Statistics, *Population Increase in the U.A.R. and its Deterrents to Development* (Cairo, 1966) Table 64, p. 150.
1970: *Statistical Abstract of the A.R.E.* (Cairo, June 1972).

inter-war years and during the Second World War when imports were in scarce supply. It was only after the Revolution, however, that import substitution policies were strongly encouraged. Unfortunately, owing to the uncertainties prevailing in the 1950s, private investors were very reluctant to put up capital even for the expansion of existing industries such as textiles. There was no question of local entrepreneurs raising sufficient capital for the establishment of a steel industry, for example, as Nasser wanted. Local businessmen were in fact more ready to invest outside Egypt altogether at this time, and the authorities had to actually impose controls on the export of capital. Given this dearth of local finance, the Government had little choice but to become a major investor itself.

The state adopted comprehensive economic planning policies by the late 1950s, and drew up a 10-year plan for development. The first phase ran from 1960–65, and the second phase up to 1970. One of the main aims of this plan was to build up basic heavy industry, especially iron and steel, chemicals and electricity. It was realised that enormous investment expenditure would be necessary and that direct returns would be low. The increase in the volume of output per unit of additional investment is low in agriculture, industry and services, though higher in construction as Table 3.5 indicates. These figures take account only of the marginal efficiency (or productivity) of capital in particular sectors, however, and ignore externalities. Investment in electricity generation, for example, not only results in returns to that industry, it can also ensure cheap and plentiful power supplies for the rest of industry. State investment plans can take account of these kinds of externalities, whereas private investors only take account of financial costs and returns to the particular industry. The Egyptian authorities wanted to establish basic industries, as it was realised these would create more favourable conditions for self-sustaining industrial growth and would complement development in other sectors of the economy. Heavy industries such as iron and steel have forward linkages to light industries such as electronics, vehicle assembly and consumer durable manufacture. The chemical industry has close linkages with the agricultural sector, as it provides farm inputs such as fertiliser and insecticides.

The establishment of this heavy industrial base should help to ensure the success of Egypt's new 'Open Door' policy, outlined by President Sadat recently.[17] With the rapid increase in petroleum prices as a consequence of the events of October 1973, there is now a massive surplus of Arab oil revenue available for investment. Egypt hopes to attract a large share of this capital for industrial development, and investment guarantees on remission of profits are now being offered. Large amounts of investment funds from government sources—including Saudi Arabia, Kuwait, Iran and the United States—have now been pledged.[18] It is also hoped to attract private funds, especially from the Gulf region. The fact that Egypt already has an established industrial base as a consequence of the policies pursued during the 1950s and 1960s should help to ensure there are fewer teething problems with new industries established. In addition, as new developments can benefit from the externalities already existing in lower Egypt, this should enable a high rate of return of private investment from overseas to be realised. The new 'Open Door' policy does not represent an ideological turn around because, as already pointed out, conditions were such in the last decade that the state had little choice but to play a major role in industrial development. Now that conditions have changed, and private capital is available, pragmatic considerations mean that it would be unwise for the Egyptian authorities not to endeavour to attract investment from these sources.

It is not surprising that Egypt's infant industries should have experienced so many difficulties in the first few years. Costs per unit of output were high. The cost of assembling a Fiat car in Egypt for example (locally called a Nasr) is still much greater than the cost of making the same model in Italy, even though wages and salaries are much lower in Egypt's motor industry. These high costs partly reflect an underutilisation of capacity, as the domestic market was limited. Industries such as the steel plant at Helwan were not able to produce at an output point where they could take advantage of economies of scale. In addition, it took time for the workforce to become proficient at running such modern industrial plants. There seems to have been major shortcomings in the management of many sections of Egyptian industry.[19] To some extent these shortcomings were accentuated by the system of promotion, which was not always based on merit, but too often on private and family connections. It may seem strange that such practices should exist in state-owned industries. Thus state ownership and the absence of profit motivation lead to management neglecting cost factors. Often attention was fixed on meeting production targets, with little regard being paid to how efficiently these were attained. In much of the state sector there was a considerable amount of featherbedding, as industries were obliged to accept graduates coming out of the university system, even when the firms were already overstaffed on the management side. In many industries there were too many managers and personnel in administration in relation to the number of workers actually engaged on production jobs. As senior employees were virtually immune from dismissal, there was always a temptation to seek a quiet life, rather than constantly strive to improve efficiency. Many of these facets of Egyptian industry just outlined still prevail, but the authorities have recently become increasingly aware of the shortcomings in the state sector. It is now hoped that competition from newly established private industry resulting from the 'Open Door' policy, should help to stimulate increased efficiency in the state sector.

In terms of employment creation, Egypt's industrial development programme must be regarded as disappointing. Though there have been considerable increases in output, the expansion of employment opportunities in manufacturing has been slow. By 1970, 16 per cent of the enumerated workforce was engaged in industry, as Table 3.4 shows. Yet 60 years earlier, the proportion was as high as 10 per cent. Admittedly it would be unwise to read too much into figures spanning such a long time period, as in 1910 only a small proportion of workforce was in enumerated employment, while most were casually employed in the informal sector. Even today only a quarter of Egypt's population is engaged in enumerated wage employment which takes no account of handicrafts. Probably as many as half the population, however, work during some period of the year, though many in agriculture are seasonally underemployed. Taking more recent figures covering enumerated employment in the 1965–70 period, it appears that there was an increase of 74,000 workers engaged in manufacturing as Table 3.5 indicates (column 2). This increase represented less than one-fifth of the enumerated workforce growth during the period, and this proportion is probably much smaller if casual employment was taken into account. Even in enumerated wage employment, however, most new jobs were created in agriculture which still accounts for over half of the registered workforce.

   The cost of creating new jobs in industry appears to be enormous, as Table 3.5 (column 5) shows. The total amount of investment undertaken for each enumerated job created in industry amounted to L.E.7730 during the 1965–70 period. Of course, this investment will have multiplier effects, as these additional employees spend their new incomes on goods and services, which in turn leads to further employment expansion. As much of this expansion may be in the non-enumerated informal sector, it is difficult to estimate the strength of these multiplier effects. Even if the creation of each new job in industry resulted in two additional jobs being created elsewhere, which would imply a very high investment multiplier, the amount of investment per job would still be considerable —over L.E.2500—in a country where G.D.P. per capita is only L.E.88 at current prices. The cost of creating new jobs in manufacturing is almost three times greater than the investment required for each additional job created in agriculture on average, and over four times the cost of new job creation in services.

   This high level of investment required to create additional employment reflects the capital intensive nature of Egypt's industry, and the advanced technology which has been adopted. This capital intensive technology admittedly results in a high level of per capita industrial output, averaging L.E.2459 per worker during 1969–70.[20] The average gross output per capita in industry is almost nine times that of the agricultural sector, and over four times that in the service sector as Table 3.5 (column 7) indicates. This high labour productivity enables high wages to be paid in industry. In fact industrial wages are over three times higher than agricultural wages, as column 8 of the table shows.

   The question arises whether the choice of capital intensive industrial techniques was appropriate for Egypt, given the high cost of capital and

TABLE 3.5. Employment and investment in Egypt

Sector	(1) Numbers employed 1969–70 ('000)	(2) Increase in employment 1965–70 ('000)	(3) % increase in employment 1965–70	(4) Investment per sector 1965–70 (L.E. millions)	(5) Investment per job created 1965–70 (L.E.)	(6) Investment per additional unit of output 1965–70	(7) Output per capita 1969–70 (L.E.)	(8) Wages per capita 1969–70 (L.E.)
Agriculture	4048	171	4·4	447	2614	0·43	266	54
Industry	916	74	12·4	572	7730	0·84	2459	192
Electricity	23	4	23·2	242	60,500	0·06	2649	276
Construction	388	60	18·3	18	300	3·78	685	185
Services	2900	358	14·1	621	1735	0·55	570	244

Note: Employment data covers only enumerated wage employment and excludes jobs in the 'informal' sector.
Source: Central Agency for Public Mobilisation and Statistics. Figures given above computed from basic data in the *Statistical Handbook*, June 1972.

the large and growing available labour pool. The output of Egyptian industry per unit of investment is low even by Third World standards. The returns to capital invested appears to be almost twice as high in the agricultural sector as column 6 of Table 3.5 indicates. Thus, whereas in industry it requires 0·84 units of capital to produce an additional unit of output, in agriculture only 0·43 units are needed for an equivalent unit of output measured in value terms, according to the author's assessment using Egyptian official government statistics. Would the adoption of more labour intensive intermediate technological processes raise the returns on scarce[21] capital and, in addition, provide more employment opportunities? Given Egypt's factor endowment the case for the adoption of intermediate technology would seem to be a strong one.

The choice facing Egypt can be presented very strikingly in diagrammatic form. The production isoquant in Figure 2 illustrates alternative

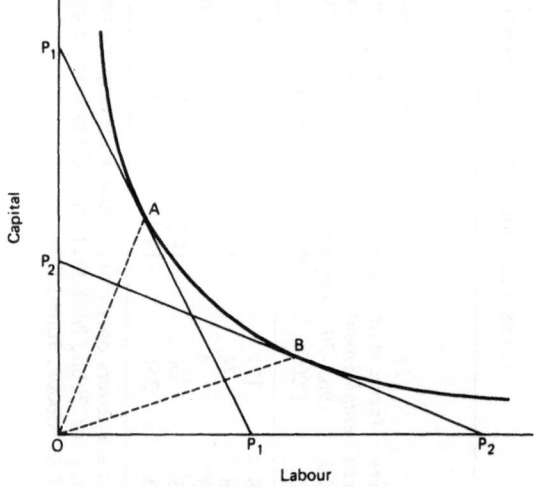

FIG. 2. Choice of techniques

methods of undertaking one industrial process. At points A and B output is the same, but at A the industry uses less labour and more capital than at B. The factor intensities are as illustrated by the dashed rays OA and OB. The lines tangential to the isoquant represent relative factor prices, with P_1 depicting the situation in a developed country where capital is plentiful and cheap, and labour scarce, while P_2 represents the situation in a country such as Egypt, where labour is cheap, and capital scarce and expensive. Egypt's industrial strategy in the 1950s and 1960s resulted in the adoption of capital intensive methods of production corresponding to the ray OA. However, given Egypt's resource endowment, and relative factor prices, it might have been more appropriate to adopt methods of production corresponding to OB. With some industries, admittedly, such a choice may not be possible. All methods of steel production for example are capital intensive. With textiles, however, one of Egypt's major industries, this is not the case. If Egyptian government policy had given priority to the objective of employment creation, this would have therefore affected not only the choice of technique within particular industries, but also the range of industries adopted. Where intermediate technology substitution is impossible, inter-industry substitution may be the only alternative.[22]

PROGRESS WITH IMPORT SUBSTITUTION IN IRAN

Iran, the second country selected for a case study of import substitution, displays economic features which differ sharply from those of Egypt. Both countries are comparable in terms of population size, while their traditional patterns of economic activity are also alike, and this is reflected in the similar level of basic skills of the local workforce in each state. The main contrast, however, is that Iran has abundant capital resources to finance its development expenditure because of its oil wealth, but Egypt is desperately short of funds for investment, and uses up a large part of its foreign exchange earnings paying service charges on the debts incurred in purchasing military equipment. Iran's oil revenues have helped to promote import substitution, both directly through state run industry, especially in the capital goods sector, and indirectly by financing incentives to private firms mostly involved in light manufacturing.[23] The rise in petroleum revenues in 1974 resulted in the Fifth Development Plan (1973/74–77/78) being expanded so that the fixed investment envisaged now amounts to $68,600 million, of which $45,400 million will be contributed by the public sector, and the remainder privately. Such enormous expenditure will undoubtedly widen the local market for import substitutes to an enormous extent, especially when multiplier effects are taken into account as those working on the projects spend their earnings. In fact gross national product is expected to rise at the startling rate of 25 per cent per annum at fixed prices, which will result in the per capita income increasing from its 1973 level of only $556 to an estimated $1521 by 1978. This will put living standards in Iran on a par with those of many European countries and means that by then the market will be comparable to that of Spain, for example.

During the last decade the expansion of Iranian manufacturing activity has been very rapid as Table 3.6 shows, with output rising almost five times between 1962 and 1972. The increase in employment was much less spectacular, however, for, even by the end of the period, less than two million people were engaged in manufacturing. This disappointing increase in industrial employment was largely a consequence of the capital intensive nature of most of the new plants which were set up to produce import substitutes. The Iranian experience has been similar to that of Egypt as far as employment is concerned, with massive amounts of investment creating only a relatively small number of additional jobs. The cost of creating each new job in Iranian industry now averages £8500, an amount which is comparable to the cost of job creation in many types of industrial activity in western Europe. Industrial production is concentrated in large expensive plants which account for two-thirds of the total value added in manufacturing, as Table 3.6 shows. Over half the total industrial workforce works in small establishments, however, employing under 50 people; and most of these in fact are really workshops with less than 10 people engaged, including the owner.[24] There has been relatively little investment in these small establishments despite their significance for employment, as most new industrial projects are on a large scale, necessitating vast amounts of investment expenditure. This is reflected in the rapidly increasing sums allocated to investment illustrated by Table 3.6; during the 1963–72 decade, investment in manufacturing industry increased sevenfold. The rise in the rate of investment has exceeded the increase in both output and value added, which indicates that the rate of return on investment is steadily decreasing. This is hardly surprising, however, given the shortages of skilled labour and other factors such as managerial expertise, which results in rapidly diminishing returns to the abundant factor, capital.

Import substitution in Iran has occurred at all stages of manufacturing production, and has not only included final consumer products, but also intermediate and capital goods. Domestic production has risen most rapidly as a proportion of the domestic market in the field of consumer durable and capital goods, as Table 3.7 shows, with Iran's own firms gaining an additional 25 per cent of the domestic market during

TABLE 3.6. Changes in Iranian manufacturing industry

	Output ('000 million rials)	Value added ('000 million rials)	Investment ('000 million rials)	Employment ('000)	Share of large units in total value added (%)
1962	77·6	33·6	6·6	1083	55
1963	89·7	38·5	5·1	1070	57
1964	105·6	42·2	6·8	1103	61
1965	153·3	48·4	10·5	1170	75
1966	177·5	56·0	16·0	1252	70
1967	226·6	68·0	19·3	1335	67
1968	252·9	77·1	30·0	1402	68
1969	276·2	86·6	39·3	1468	66
1970	304·2	95·0	45·1	1543	65
1971	343·3	107·1	49·4	1625	65
1972	379·7	122·1	52·4	1820	67

Note: Figures in real terms. Price deflations undertaken by Mohamed Yamin, formerly at Durham University, from data in Bank Markazi Annual Reports and Balance Sheets, 1349 (1970–71) p. 150, and 1351 (1972–73) p. 180.

Sources: Ministry of Economy, *Statistics on Large Industrial Establishments of Iran in 1969*, p. viii; Ministry of Economy, *Iranian Industrial Statistics for 1350 (1971–1972)*, pp. 'kh'–'d' (in Persian); Ministry of Economy, *Iranian Industrial Statistics for 1351 (1972–1973)*, pp. 21–22 and p. 26 (in Persian); International Labour Office, *Employment and Income Policies for Iran*, p. 31.

TABLE 3.7. Significance of import substitution in Iran

Industry	Domestic production as a proportion of domestic market (%)			Distribution of the Growth of manufacturing output between import substitutes and demand expansion components (%) 1960–72	
	1960	*1969*	*Change 1960–69 (%)*	*Import substitutes*	*Demand expansion*
Consumer non-durable	92·8	99·4	+ 6·6	25·0	75·0
Food and beverages	87·6	98·9	+11·3	21·3	78·7
Tobacco	100·0	100·0	0·0	—	—
Textiles	98·0	100·8	+ 2·8	21·0	79·0
Apparel	86·7	100·1	+13·4	5·9	94·1
Wood and furniture	77·7	75·6	− 2·1	51·9	48·1

Intermediate	37·3	54·9	+17·6	63·7	36·2
Paper	31·5	52·6	+21·1	⎱ 63·0	37·0
Printing	28·4	93·7	+65·3	⎰	
Rubber	16·0	59·5	+43·5	84·0	16·0
Chemicals	25·1	55·9	+30·8	74·0	26·0
Basic metal and metal products	31·2	38·3	+ 7·1	72·4	26·6
Non-metallic minerals	81·1	82·4	+ 1·3	25·0	75·0
Consumer durables and capital	17·3	42·5	+25·2	72·7	27·3
Machinery	0·8	6·9	+ 6·1	92·9	7·1
Electrical equipment	4·9	38·5	+33·6	89·5	10·5
Transport	39·7	70·9	+31·2	53·6	46·4
Miscellaneous	19·4	83·9	+64·5	55·0	44·4
Total	59·9	73·9	+14·0	54·6	45·4

Note: The average figures for each group (consumer non-durable, intermediate, and consumer durable and capital goods) are weighted for domestic production as a proportion of the domestic market by the contribution to output of the individual sector. Average figures for demand expansion and import substitution components are unweighted, however.

Sources: Output data from Ministry of Economy, *Iranian Industrial Statistics for 1349 (1970–71)*, pp. 53–90; and 1351 (1972–73), pp. 52–71. Import data from United Nations, *International Trade Statistics*, 1960, pp. 291; Ministry of Economy, *Input-Output of Iranian Import and Export (1962–1970)*, pp. 8–31.

the 1960–69 period. This huge increase is of course largely explained by the fact that domestic production of consumer durables and capital goods was very limited in 1960, with only a small range of products manufactured, in contrast to consumer non-durables, over nine-tenths of which were supplied domestically even at that time. These consumer non-durables included items such as textiles, clothing and furniture, most of which were produced in the small workshop establishments already mentioned. The food processing, bottling and tobacco plants tended to be somewhat larger, and used more modern methods of production.[25]

It is these consumer non-durable goods produced for a mass low-income market that usually are the first import substitutes manufactured locally in Third World countries. The fixed costs of production are quite low for such goods because the machinery required for manufacturing is relatively simple. In addition, output can be varied easily to meet changing demand conditions; and there are few indivisibilities in production, though no significant economies of scale either. The scope for expansion in these fields was limited in Iran even by 1960, however, as the local market was already saturated with domestically produced non-durable goods. Market prospects seemed much more promising for consumer durables, especially with rising incomes, as the income elasticity of demand is high for these goods, but low for consumer non-durables. The growing middle classes want durable goods such as cars, televisions, refrigerators, washing machines, etc., items often regarded as essentials in the more affluent suburbs of Tehran and the other major cities. Table 3.7 illustrates the extent to which Iranian industry has met the challenge of this growing local market, as domestically produced electrical equipment accounted for under 5 per cent of the market in 1960, but its share had risen to almost 40 per cent of a much larger market by 1969. The expansion in vehicle assembly has been equally remarkable as by 1969 local plants supplied over 70 per cent of the market, compared with under 40 per cent in 1960. The American Chrysler company has a virtual monopoly of all local production, and it assembles imported Hillman components manufactured by the company's United Kingdom subsidiary.[26]

There has been little import substitution of capital goods such as machinery in Iran, and imports still account for over 90 per cent of the domestic market. This is, perhaps, not surprising as the techniques involved in manufacturing capital goods are highly sophisticated, and require a high level of skill and technical knowledge.[27] In addition, the market for machinery in Iran is clearly limited in spite of the boom in consumer durables. Even in the advanced economies of western Europe, such as Germany, France or Britain, a large proportion of such goods are imported, as countries often specialise in one particular type of machinery, to get a long production run, and export this product, which helps to pay for the import of other capital goods not made domestically. Progress in Iran with local production of intermediate goods has been much more rapid, especially products such as paper, printing, rubber and chemicals. A large proportion of the chemicals made locally are byproducts of the petroleum industry. The decade 1960–69 saw only limited expansion in the manufacture of intermediate goods such as metal products or non-metallic minerals, although domestic producers did manage to slightly increase their share of the local market. The steel industry has expanded rapidly in the 1970s, however, and it is expected that output will reach 10 million tons a year by 1978. The giant steel mill at Isfahan established under an Irano-Russian economic agreement is now in full production, and the machine fabricating plant at Arak has been producing steel pipes for several years now. Iran's steel industry appears to have experienced much fewer teething problems than that of Egypt.

In Table 3.7 an attempt is made to divide the growth of industrial output into import substitution and demand expansion components using a method developed by Chenery.[28] The demand expansion component is that part of output growth which is due to increased domestic or foreign demand for products from an industry, either by consumers or by the final producers where capital goods are being made. Chenery's import substitution component is measured as that part of the growth of output which is due to a decline in the share of imports to the total supply of the industry. Using this method the results appear to confirm those presented in the first two columns of the table. The import substitution component is highest for machinery and electrical goods, most of which are consumer durables. Around nine-tenths of the expansion in output of these goods can be attributed directly to import substitution. For non-durable items such as food, beverages, textiles and clothing, the import substitution component over the 1960–72 period was relatively low, because Iran was already a major producer of such goods at the start of the period, and imported only small quantities.[29]

The degree of state control over industry in Iran, however, is much less than in Egypt, although in both countries heavy industry is nationalised. In Iran, as in Egypt, the motive for state intervention has been pragmatic rather than ideological. The state sector in manufacturing only includes industries where the amounts of capital required are so great, and the pay-off period so distant, that private investors are unlikely to take the risks. The nationalised industries have been allowed to recruit as many workers as they require to man the production processes, but there has been no compulsion to take on extra labour merely to reduce national unemployment and underemployment as in Egypt. Encouragement has been given to the private sector as much as possible, and investors have never had their assets nationalised, as happened in Egypt under Nasser. Instead there have been generous tax concessions, including tax holidays, and cheap loans have been made available to help investment. The only class of people who had assets expropriated in Iran were the large landowners, and these were adequately compensated for any losses. Many of the landowners used the compensation they received to invest in industry, although much of the money went into the construction of apartments and houses rather than industry.

Import substitution in Iran has to a large extent followed the classic pattern of the growth of consumer non-durables first, then the expansion of durable goods manufacture, and finally the creation of intermediate and capital goods industries. For centuries the country has traditionally produced goods such as clothing and footwear, and these can scarcely be considered as import substitutes. The 1960s marked the start of the consumer durables era, as already indicated, and this was when the most rapid expansion of import substitution really got under way. Of late the main development has been the spread of import substitution into the intermediate and capital goods sector, although at the same time some of the tariff protection for the older-established consumer-orientated industries has been reduced. This has been done partly because the government felt these industries were becoming mature, and were in a position to withstand foreign competition. At the same time it was hoped that this outside competition would encourage Iranian firms to keep down prices, which would help reduce the inflationary pressures the economy had experienced as a result of the boom of the mid-1970s following the oil revenue increases.

Although Iran has been fortunate in having abundant oil resources, the links between the petroleum sector and the rest of the economy have been extremely tenuous. The oil sector has admittedly provided the finance for the development of industry, but its demand for domestically produced goods has remained low in comparison to imports, as Table 3.8 shows.[30] In 1961 the consortium of private oil companies operating in Iran purchased less than one-seventh of their requirements domestically, and by 1968 the proportion obtained locally was still

TABLE 3.8. Value of purchases by oil companies 1961–68

Year	Domestic products (million rials)		Imported goods (million rials)		Imports as proportion of total purchases (%)	
	NIOC	Consortium	NIOC	Consortium	NIOC	Consortium
1961	57	535	474	3712	89	87
1962	92	485	497	3585	84	88
1963	95	438	417	2552	81	85
1964	106	420	460	5080	81	92
1965	148	493	521	8939	78	95
1966	107	507	797	3261	88	87
1967	153	538	1067	4327	87	89
1968	188	693	985	3618	84	84

Source: *National Iranian Oil Company Annual Report 1968.*

below one-sixth. Ironically, the state-owned National Iranian Oil Company purchased even less domestically, as only one-eighth of its requirements were locally supplied in 1961, and one-sixth in 1968, the consortium level. Yet as NIOC is the third largest company of any type in the world outside the United States, with sales of almost $17,000 million annually, its purchasing power is enormous. The company is not only involved in oil drilling, but also owns refineries, pipelines, tankers, vast petrochemical complexes, gas processing plants, etc.[31] Through these downstream investments it accounts for a major proportion of Iran's total capital goods imports. State ownership has clearly done little to increase the impact of petroleum expenditures on the country's economy, and local multiplier effects on income remain limited.

DIVERSIFICATION IN PERSPECTIVE

From these case studies of import substitution in Egypt and Iran several conclusions emerge which may be of interest in those Middle Eastern states where economic diversification through such policies is only just beginning. First, the teething problems which the new industries experienced in both countries were much greater than anticipated, and in most cases the suspicions of private investors concerning the initial lack of economic viability for the projects was probably well-founded. In both Egypt and Iran, the state was forced to play a major role in the industrialisation process, despite initial reluctance in Egypt, and a continuing government commitment in Iran to create an economic environment which favours domestic private enterprise.

The second problem which both case studies highlight is that of employment. In both countries the proportion of the population engaged in industry has only increased slightly despite the vast investment expenditures. Iran is admittedly in a much more fortunate position than Egypt with regard to the availability of finance, but even there it must be asked whether greater economic progress could have been made if more resources had been directed into the agricultural sector and rural craft industries, rather than into large-scale projects. In the two countries it has largely been the urban middle classes who have benefited most from the development strategy pursued, while the rural areas remain neglected backwaters for the most part.

A major objective of import substitution policy is to save foreign exchange, and consequently help a country's balance of payments. In the cases of Egypt and Iran, however, the converse has been the case, as the development of new industries has increased the import bill in both countries, and aggravated their balance of payments problems. As already mentioned, the industries established in the two countries have been highly capital intensive, and most of the expensive new plant and machinery is imported from the advanced industrial nations of the Communist world and the West. In addition, many of the new plants in fields such as consumer durables are assembly operations only, and the components continue to be imported. The proportion of value added in manufacture abroad in car assembly for example in Iran and Egypt, was greater than the value added locally in the initial stages of production. This situation has now changed, fortunately, but in the early stages the multinational companies involved in setting up the car plants gained more than the two host countries, as they had a virtual monopoly of the local markets for their components. Clearly governments in the Middle East adopting import substitution policies need to consider carefully what level of tariff protection to grant, so that their domestic consumers do not lose too much through the consequent market distortions. The issue of tariff and exchange rate policies will be explored more fully in the next chapter.

4 Tariff and Exchange
   Rate Policies

Although the Middle East as a whole maintains a large payments surplus with the rest of the world, there is a maze of controls over trade
and currency contractions. It is ironic that controls are so widespread,
while at the same time there is much debate about the capacity of the
leading Middle East trading nations to absorb imports; and the issue
of petro-currency recycling still figures prominently in the financial
news. Even the richest oil-producing states, such as Kuwait, have general
import licensing systems which apply to all goods apart from foodstuffs.[1]
Admittedly these licences are at present easy to obtain for most manufactured goods, but as Kuwait starts diversifying its economy and
establishing new industry, the range of prohibited imports is becoming
greater. Clearly, even where Middle Eastern countries have huge
foreign exchange reserves, and large balance of payments surpluses,
quotas and tariffs may still be adopted as a means of protecting infant
industries. Indeed, in so far as the existence of payments surpluses
enables countries to industrialise rapidly, those countries in the most
favourable foreign exchange position may be the ones which introduce
the greatest range of import restrictions during the next few years.

   It is convenient to classify the countries of the Middle East into two
groups with regard to the motivation behind foreign trade restrictions.[2]
The first group comprises the major Arab oil-exporting states, which,
as in the case of Kuwait, adopted trade restrictions mainly as a means
to promote import substitution. Iran does not fall into this category
because, although it has enjoyed a large payments surplus since the oil
price rises of 1974, the import requirements of its large population have
resulted in foreign exchange difficulties being experienced there in the
past. The Iranian authorities therefore proceed with caution with regard
to trade questions, and review their import control policy from year to
year, monitoring carefully at the same time the changes in their balance

of payments position. Thus Iran is probably best classed with those Middle Eastern countries such as Egypt or Syria which impose import controls primarily for the sake of the balance of payments.[3] All three countries spend a considerable proportion of their foreign exchange earnings on imported armaments which heightens the need for controls.

The history of controls on trade varies widely from country to country in the Middle East. Iran and Turkey have exercised some form of import control for more than five hundred years, usually in the form of customs duties. Originally these duties were levied as a means of raising government revenue, as there was no system of income tax in the Middle East. It was much easier administratively to impose a tax on traded goods, as most import consignments were handled by a few ports. Smuggling, admittedly, was a major problem, and many of the states in the Gulf thrived as centres for pirate ships involved in trading gold and other precious metals.[4] Despite this illegal activity, which the Ottomans and the Iranians were never able to stamp out, the problems in raising revenue in this way were much fewer than they would have been if direct taxes were applied to income. It would have been impossible to obtain any accurate assessment of personal or business incomes because most people kept no proper accounts. The rich, in any case, would have strongly resisted any attempt to curtail their incomes, and they constituted a politically powerful group. Clearly in the primarily agrarian economies of the Middle East some form of land tax would have been the most fruitful source of revenue; but the landlords of both the Ottoman Empire and Iran were strong enough to prevent the successful implementation of any taxation of this sort.

NOMINAL AND EFFECTIVE PROTECTION

The degree of protection which tariffs give is often seriously underestimated if account is taken only of the actual level of duty levied.[5] In practice most Middle Eastern states have tariffs which escalate according to the degree of processing involved in producing the imported goods. Thus raw materials usually enter free of duty, or are even subsidised, while the average tariff imposed on imports of manufactured final products is high, in order to encourage the establishment of local processing plants. Suppose, for example, a 100 per cent duty is levied on car imports into Egypt but car components enter free of duty, even though these components account for 50 per cent of the value added in production. In this instance the level of protection granted to Egypt's car assembly plants is 200 per cent of the value of production, twice the value of the nominal tariff. This is what is meant by the effective rate of protection which benefits the local infant industry. The benefit has to be paid for by domestic consumers, however, who must spend more to purchase the higher cost domestic goods, which are often of poorer quality than substitutes available in world markets.

High domestic prices in newly established infant industries may reflect the limited extent of the domestic market and a consequent inability to take advantage of economies of scale until the firms can build up market outlets abroad. The high level of costs may also reflect local inexperience in running modern technologically advanced plants, as already mentioned in the previous chapter on import substitution. A further problem for domestic consumers, however, is that the local protected producer will have a certain degree of monopolistic power in price determination, and this will be directly related to the size of the tariff. This is the main reason why infant industry protection should not be granted for a long period, otherwise the consumers will not profit from the industry reaching maturity. In both Egypt and Iran the local textile and clothing industries have been protected for over 40 years, long enough it must be imagined for any infant to reach maturity. There can be no economic justification for consumers paying an inflated price, and producers maintaining high cost levels for a period of this length. This is especially the case in textile production, which is suited to labour abundant economies with a low level of managerial skill. The industry is by nature labour intensive, with relatively unsophisticated manufacturing techniques.

The most detailed analysis on estimating effective rates of protection in the Middle East from nominal tariff rates has been carried out in Iran, where figures are available on a sectoral basis.[6] These results are presented in Table 4.1, which covers a wide range of manufacturing activities from food processing to capital goods industries such as machinery and metal products. The average tariff level is highest for imported beverages, especially alcoholic drinks, and tobacco, both of which constitute a major source of government revenue. Tariff levels are also high for clothes, leather and footwear, and furniture, which helps protect local manufacturers of these consumer products. The tariff level tends to be lower for raw materials such as chemicals and basic metals, although it is higher for intermediate products, which include machinery, metal products and transport equipment.

These figures for average tariff levels do not provide an accurate picture of the average level of protection. This is given in the next

TABLE 4.1. Structure of Iranian tariffs on industrial products

Industrial group	Average nominal tariff rate (%)	Average nominal rate of protection (%)	Average effective rate of protection (%)
Food processing	121	16	22
Beverages	352	157	115
Tobacco	239	249	274
Chemicals	58	95	111
Leather and footwear	179	62	434
Furniture	126	N/A	N/A
Paper and printing	12	11	−2
Rubber products	55	53	82
Textiles	90	57	74
Clothing	144	N/A	N/A
Non-metallic minerals	82	30	28
Basic metals	19	31	24
Metal products	43	47	50
Machinery	30	46	61
Vehicles	71	106	866

Source: United Nations Economic Commission for Asia and the Far East, *Effective Protection and Interregional Trade*, Vol. II, pp. 70–1.

column of the table, which measures the effect of protection on domestic industries. It is obvious that a high tariff level will have no protective effect unless there is actually a local plant to manufacture the goods in question. The values given are calculated using the formula[7]

$$\frac{OD_n - OW_n}{OW_n}$$

where OD_n = values of output of industry group n at domestic prices and OW_n = value of output of industry group n at world prices. This measure serves as an index of the level of average protection, because when there is no domestic production there is of course no protection. Where a domestic plant is established the value of its output is deflated by the appropriate tariff rate, estimated by the difference between domestic and world prices. This measure shows a high average nominal level of protection for Iranian chemical producers and vehicle manufacture (mainly cars), as might be expected. The level of protection given to the Iranian textile industry, as well as machinery and rubber products (mainly tyres), is also substantial.

In the final column of Table 4.1, the level of effective protection is given for Iranian industry. As the proportion of value added locally in industries such as vehicles is relatively small, with only low levels of duty applied to imported components, the level of effective protection is astronomical at 866 per cent, well above the level quoted for Egypt in the numerical example cited earlier. Effective protection is also high for local leather and footwear manufacturers, but much lower in industries such as food processing. Producers of raw materials enjoy little effective protection, as the figure for basic metals shows, but intermediate producers of chemicals, metal products and machinery are protected to a much greater extent. Effective protection rates therefore tend to escalate, like the rates of nominal protection, for final stage manufacturing processes. The Iranian authorities believe that these industries must be encouraged first, and then at a later stage when domestic demand for intermediate products has built up, more encouragement will be given to producers establishing themselves in this field.

The range of protective duties in Saudi Arabia is much less restrictive, as might be expected, given that the country is an even larger oil producer than Iran but has a population only a fraction of the size. This oil-surplus kingdom grants tariff protection to 29 local infant industries, most of which manufacture consumer non-durables.[8] These include items such as detergents, paper handkerchiefs and chocolate, where imported goods are subject to 20 per cent duty. Cars and commercial vehicles enter with only a 3 per cent tariff, and there are no duties payable on imported machinery or capital equipment. In 1975, however, a joint venture company was set up, Saudi Arabian Motors, in which General Motors of Detroit hold 60 per cent of the capital, with 40 per cent subscribed in Saudi Arabia. This new company has been licensed to assemble 7800 vehicles a year, including Chevrolet trucks, a small number of buses, and Torana cars, a highly successful Australian model. It is expected that tariff protection will be given to the new company's vehicles, probably on a comparable level to that prevailing in Iran for local vehicle assembly plants. As a consequence the parent company, General Motors, hopes the value of its exports to Saudi Arabia will actually rise after the opening of its subsidiary, as it expects that it will increase its market share, which would mean greater sales of American vehicle components.[9]

Although, therefore, in Saudi Arabia the number of commodities subject to import duty is limited at present, as the country develops new infant industries the range of tariffs is likely to be extended considerably. Undoubtedly this will largely affect consumer durables in the first instance, which will enjoy a high degree of effective protection, as intermediate and capital goods continue to enter free of duty for the foreseeable future. Such a tariff policy, as in Iran, should do much to encourage expansion of infant industries in fields where there is a reasonable local market. The scope for domestic capital or intermediate goods manufacture in Saudi Arabia seems much less promising, despite the country's ambitious plans for the steel industry. Any tariff protection on steel may only serve to lower the effective protection given to consumer goods industries, and lower their prospects of profitability.

Despite the trend away from free trade in the Middle East as more countries attempt to diversify their economies, there are some countervailing forces at work, the Arab Common Market being the most notable. Its effect on trade patterns will be dealt with in detail in the next chapter. A further factor encouraging trade has been the subsidies introduced on food imports by Saudi Arabia and the Gulf states, which in effect constitute a type of negative tariff. They were brought in basically as an anti-inflation measure to augment available food supplies and keep down internal prices.[10] In practice, because they also help to reduce wage pressure by lowering the rate of cost of living increase, these subsidies have the effect of increasing the rate of effective protection for domestic industry, especially in fields where production processes are relatively labour intensive. As far as local agriculture is concerned, however, the effect of the import subsidies is inevitably detrimental. Nevertheless, as the countries involved are in an arid region, with little domestic agriculture, any adverse impact is minimal, especially where local farmers are highly subsidised as well.

One major Middle East country which has been liberalising its trade policy recently is Egypt. Under Nasser the country adopted stringent import controls and imposed high tariff levels in order to protect the newly established infant industries; but since 1973 the pendulum has swung the other way, against the general trend towards restrictions in the Middle East. Under the new 'Open Door' policy, which was approved by the Egyptian parliament in 1974, free zones were created in certain regions of the country, including most of the Suez Canal area. Companies establishing themselves in this free zone are allowed to import capital and intermediate goods without paying any import duties. In this way it is hoped to encourage new industrial development in the Suez Canal cities which were largely devastated in the 1967 conflict with

Israel, but which are being rebuilt following the 1973 war gains. This policy makes significant concessions; Egypt's tariffs on machinery are normally 25 per cent, and where equipment is produced locally, as is the case with steel, import duty is as high as 40 per cent. Imported consumer durables, however, are subject to nominal tariff levels of up to 200 per cent; so with these concessions on imported inputs, the rate of effective protection granted in the Suez Canal area should be enormous.[11] It is hoped that many of the new industries established will produce for export markets and thus earn Egypt useful foreign exchange; but the industries would only have a price advantage in these markets in so far as competitors in other countries have to pay tariffs on their imported inputs. A more readily accessible market may in fact be within the Canal Zone itself, as those engaged in transit trade spend their earnings. The value of this spending to Egypt may be several times the actual Canal dues charged on shipping.[12] At the time of writing it must be said that the fruits of this trade liberalisation policy have been disappointing in terms of new industries actually established, despite the high level of effective protection. The situation may change if the Egyptian economy picks up, and if there are the necessary income effects to complement the price incentives which the country's tariff policy provides.

DIRECT IMPORT CONTROLS

Many of the countries of the Middle East have adopted some system of import licensing whereby prospective importers have to apply to the government for permission to purchase foreign goods. The major exceptions to this policy are Saudi Arabia and Gulf States such as Qatar, Bahrain, Oman and the United Arab Emirates. In these countries there are no quantitative restrictions on imports, apart from goods from Israel, where the Arab boycott applies, and imports from Rhodesia which are prohibited under the United Nations sanctions policy. Imports of alcoholic beverages are not allowed in these countries, apart from Bahrain, although some of the other Gulf states import small amounts for sale to expatriates in hotels. Oman extends this prohibition to soft drinks in order to give the local bottling industry complete protection.[13] Despite their oil surpluses, both Kuwait and Libya have a general licensing system on imports and therefore cannot be classified with those states already mentioned. In both states the policy has been introduced to ensure that imports are handled mainly by registered dealers, who must be either local citizens or companies of which a majority of the stock is held domestically. Both governments hope this policy will ensure that import policy is in the national interest, and the registration of dealers facilitates the introduction of any further direct controls deemed necessary. Importers, other than registered dealers, must apply to the appropriate ministry for permission to import each specific item. A similar system is in operation in Iraq.

Iran, despite its oil surpluses in recent years, has a much more comprehensive system of direct controls on imports.[14] Import policy is re-examined annually and an 'Import List' is published each year by the Ministry of Commerce. This list distinguishes between 'authorised', 'unauthorised' and 'prohibited' goods. 'Authorised' goods consist of items which are not produced in Iran, or produced in insufficient quantity given local market requirements. These goods comprise mainly capital and intermediate products, the importation of which is considered essential for the country's development. 'Unauthorised' items comprise mainly consumer durables and non-durables, which are produced domestically in sufficient quantity for local needs, and whose importation is deemed to be non-essential. There is a considerable amount of bureaucracy involved in Iran's import control system, as importers have to pay a registration fee equivalent to 1 per cent of the value of the imports and, in addition, for many non-food items, a 15 per cent import deposit is charged. This is payable to the Central Bank, but will be refunded once customs clearance is obtained. Needless to say, these procedures can cause considerable delays, even with the importation of essential 'authorised' goods.

Countries in persistent foreign exchange difficulties, such as Egypt, Syria and Israel, have even more rigorous controls on imports, as might be expected. Although Egypt does not impose import quotas on particular items at the start of each financial year, each sector of the economy is allocated an overall quota of foreign exchange which it can use for import payments.[15] The total hard currency funds available are determined by the residual from visible export earnings and invisibles, after all servicing charges have been met on previous debt commitments. In Egypt's case these servicing charges of foreign loans are extremely high, owing to the huge debt incurred in the purchase of military equipment from the Soviet Union and elsewhere. Although most of the payments to the Soviet Union have been made in the form of goods rather than foreign exchange, owing to the barter nature of the trade deals, there is still an opportunity cost in terms of hard currency, since goods provided to make these payments, such as cotton or textiles, cannot be exported elsewhere to earn foreign exchange.[16]

The import controls imposed by Syria are as stringent as those of Egypt, but the actual trade formalities are somewhat different—which must add to the confusion of any prospective exporter hoping to sell goods in a range of Middle East countries. As well as having a 'prohibited' list of imports basically designed to protect local industries, Syria also places many items on a 'suspended' list. Importation of many consumer durables has been halted temporarily because of the country's balance of payments difficulties since the October 1973 war, and this ban even applies to some intermediate and capital goods. Specific items included in this list can only be imported if permission is obtained from the Ministry of Economy and Foreign Trade, and licences are only available in exceptional circumstances. One unique feature of Syrian controls is the stipulation that goods must be purchased directly from the country of origin rather than through an intermediary. This provision was basically designed to circumvent Beirut middlemen and prevent them profiting from Syria's trade, while at the same time giving a boost to the country's own ports.

Like Syria, Israel's reserve position was also adversely affected by the October 1973 war and, as well as import surcharges, the country has also introduced more rigorous controls on the purchase of goods from abroad. Importers are required to make a special deposit at the Treasury which is equivalent to 20 per cent of the imported goods, except for foodstuffs or strategic items. These deposits are held for 1 year by the Treasury before being refunded, and no interest is payable.[17] Despite Israel's payments difficulties, importation is subject to fewer formalities than is the case in most Middle Eastern countries.

The same, unfortunately, cannot be said of Turkey, which has probably the most complex and bureaucratic system of controls in the entire region. It has adopted a system of lists similar to Israel, with essential items including many foodstuffs on a liberalised list. All other goods are subject to global quotas, which are drawn up by the Ministry of Commerce on an annual basis for particular industries, and three times a year for private commercial importers. All this involves a considerable amount of administration, which is further complicated by a system of pre-import price controls carefully devised to ensure that imports are purchased at the best ruling world market prices. A certificate must be obtained from the Office of Price Registration and Control to show this. This provision makes economic sense in theory, but in practice it is difficult for the Office to check on world prices for a vast range of commodities in a situation of global inflation. The system has therefore been temporarily suspended, but the Turkish authorities still hope to re-introduce it as soon as possible. Despite these cumbersome restrictions, trade between the European Economic Community and Turkey is booming, largely because, under an agreement between both parties, a number of community imports have been included in the liberalised list, in exchange for reciprocal concessions on Turkish exports. Community exporters therefore enjoy preferential treatment in Turkey over their competitors from elsewhere.

CURRENCY EXCHANGE SYSTEMS

The exchange rate policies adopted by the major trading nations of the Middle East are almost as varied as their system of import controls.

For example, the currencies of some of the oil-exporting nations are freely convertible, as might be expected, while countries with persistent foreign exchange problems such as Egypt, Israel and Syria place severe limits on convertibility. Six nations in the Middle East, Saudi Arabia, Kuwait, the Union of Arab Emirates, Bahrain, Qatar and Oman, formally accept the obligations of Article VIII, Sections 2, 3 and 4, of the International Monetary Fund agreement on convertibility. In practice this means these currencies can be freely converted in world money markets, which enables these countries to conduct trade easily on a multilateral basis without having to make any special currency swop arrangements.[18] Until its present crisis, Lebanon had similar arrangements, although it did not formally accept the obligations of the fund.

How the system works can be illustrated in terms of a simple example. Suppose, for instance, an exporter from the United Kingdom selling consumer durables to Kuwait agrees to accept Kuwaiti dinars as payment, the British exporter can sell these earnings to a bank in London (or any other financial centre) in exchange for sterling. Now these dinars can be used to pay for United Kingdom imports from the United States if necessary. The United States exporter will in turn be prepared to accept these dinars as payment, knowing that they can be converted freely into dollars, and perhaps eventually be used to finance America's oil imports from Kuwait. In this example, only three countries were involved, but in most cases the payments pattern will involve many nations before eventually the dinars find their way back to Kuwait again. Those Middle Eastern countries with convertible currencies therefore enjoy many advantages in trade, the main ones being flexibility with regard to import supplies and the ability to shop around to find the most suitable goods at the keenest prices. In return for this privilege, however, these countries have to maintain sufficient foreign exchange reserves to meet all the demands of those who want to convert their currency holdings. In addition, those countries with convertible currencies have to be in a strong enough reserve position to support their exchange rates, so that if there is a spate of withdrawals the downward slide will not be too marked. If this happens, confidence in the currency will be undermined and the exchange rate will fall well below the rate which the Central Bank of the country concerned wishes to maintain. Thus the Central Banks require foreign exchange for intervention purposes, which will probably be quite frequently used, in addition to the need for sufficient reserves to maintain credibility as a lender in the last resort.[19] Clearly, Saudi Arabia and the Gulf States are the only countries in the Middle East with sufficient reserves in relation to their trade to meet these requirements.

Although Iran has the second-largest holding of international reserves in the Middle East, they are much less than those of the other major oil-exporting nations of the region in relation to the total size of the country's import bill. Consequently the Iranian rial is not freely convertible and, instead, the country has bilateral payments agreements with nine of its major trading partners. Payments under the agreements with six of these countries must be made in United States dollars, but settlements with the other three trade partners, China, East Germany and North Korea, can be made in rials.[20] East German exporters, for example, can maintain non-resident accounts denominated in rials, which may be used both for payments in Iran and for conversion into foreign currency. If the holdings in these accounts are converted, however, the transaction is carried out at a non-commercial rate below the official parity for the rial. In practice, therefore, deposits in non-resident accounts are mostly used to pay for imports from Iran, usually oil and natural gas. The situation in Iraq is broadly similar with regard to non-resident accounts.

Foreign exchange payments are even more tightly circumscribed in Turkey, one of Iran's partners in the Regional Cooperation for Development. Turkey maintains bilateral payments agreements with both Iran and Pakistan through the R.C.D., and settlements are made through special accounts denominated in United States dollars. Most of Turkey's trade is with Europe, however, and the country has bilateral payments agreements with all the E.E.C. member states, with settlements going through accounts denominated in convertible Euro-currencies. Non-residents are not allowed to maintain accounts denominated in Turkish lira. This contrasts with the situation in countries such as Egypt where non-residents are allowed to hold accounts, although only those from countries that Egypt has bilateral payments arrangements with. Similar provisions apply in Syria and Israel for non-resident accounts denominated in the local currency. There are usually different categories of non-resident account, but exporters generally earn some interest on their deposits. Exporters from Egypt, Syria and Iraq are usually allowed to place their foreign exchange earnings in a special account, which can be freely converted. Foreign exporters to the three countries, however, are not necessarily accorded the same privilege, and they can easily find themselves with their earnings tied up in a blocked account. In this case the proceeds can only be spent in the country concerned. For this reason, most export contracts are awarded as part of some large bilateral trade deal, which in practice really amounts to barter.

Egypt's payments system is one of the most complex in the entire Middle East. Apart from the varying degrees of convertibility of its banking accounts, it also maintains parallel exchange markets, where different rates of conversion apply. Most exchange transactions take place at the official rate of L.E. 1 = US$2.56, but in the parallel market the exchange rate was L.E. 1 = US$1.70 buying and US$1.65 selling. Capital goods and other essential items are usually imported at the official rate, which has the effect of making these goods cheaper in the domestic market. This policy has been criticised because it constitutes a subsidy on capital and thus encourages the development of capital intensive industry which often contributes little as far as the provision of additional employment is concerned. In effect, it results in the domestic price of capital goods being relatively low in relation to wages. Indeed the high rate of conversion used in the parallel market for consumer goods may actually further raise the cost of labour, where money wages are related to the cost of living, including import prices for final goods. Tourist transactions are carried out at the rate prevailing in the parallel market, which makes holidaying Egypt much cheaper for foreign visitors than it would otherwise be.[21] Remittances from Egyptians working abroad also enter at the parallel rate, which provides a good incentive to such people to convert their savings into Egyptian pounds. This is an increasingly important source of foreign exchange for Egypt through its invisible account. Turkey maintains a similar incentive rate of exchange for remittances sent home by its workers resident abroad.

During the 1970s there has been a general upward movement in the exchange rates of most of the major currencies of the Middle East, as Table 4.2 shows. The rates quoted are against the United States dollar,

TABLE 4.2. Exchange rate policy in the Middle East

Country	Currency	Rates (U.S.$ per unit national currency)		Percentage change
		1969	1975	
Egypt	Pound L.E.	2·30	2·56	+ 11
Iran*	Rial RI	76·4	69·3	+ 9
Iraq	Dinar ID	2·80	3·38	+ 20
Israel*	Pound I£	3·50	7·10	− 103
Jordan	Dinar JD	2·80	3·03	+ 8
Kuwait	Dinar KD	2·80	3·40	+ 21
Lebanon*	Pound LL	3·25	2·30	+ 29
Libya	Dinar LD	2·80	3·38	+ 21
Qatar	Riyal QR	0·21	0·25	+ 19
Saudi Arabia*	Riyal SR	4·50	3·53	+ 21
Sudan	Pound LSd	2·87	2·45	− 15
Syria*	Pound LS	3·82	3·76	+ 2
Turkey*	Lira LT	9·0	15·2	− 31
South Yemen	Dinar YD	2·4	2·9	+ 21

Note: * Units of national currency per U.S.$.
Source: I.M.F., *International Financial Statistics*, March 1976.

however, which has declined in value since its link with gold was suspended in 1971 and it started floating. If Special Drawing Rights were taken as the *numeraire* instead of dollars, the upward shift would have been much more modest for all the countries cited. In fact Iran, Jordan and Syria have actually experienced slight depreciations in their currencies over the period in terms of Special Drawing Rights. The dollar was chosen as the *numeraire*, however, as it is the currency used by the majority of the countries listed for intervention purposes in order to maintain their rates. One new development since last year is that the Saudi Arabian riyal, the Iranian rial and the Kuwaiti dinar have been linked to Special Drawing Rights rather than dollars, which has added to the growing importance of these Rights as international units of account.[22] Nevertheless, petroleum prices are still determined in terms of dollars, despite some agitation by the OPEC nations in 1975 to have this changed to Special Drawing Rights.

The most rapidly appreciating currency in the Middle East over the 1969–75 period was the Lebanese pound, which reflects the importance of Beirut as a financial centre and the amounts of petro-currencies flowing into the coffers of its financial institutions. Unfortunately, the crisis of 1975–76 due to the conflict between Christians and Moslems in the country, has brought all this to an end. It seems unlikely that the Lebanese pound will perform in this way in the years ahead. The Saudi riyal, and the Libyan, Kuwaiti and Iraqi dinar, all rose by over one-fifth in value over the 6-year period under discussion. Partly as a consequence of this, these countries are in rather a quandary about future exchange rate policy.[23] As all four countries spend a considerable amount of foreign exchange on agricultural imports, this appreciation is at first sight welcome, especially by domestic consumers, because it helps keep down domestic food prices. Only Iraq has any significant agricultural sector and therefore needs to worry about the detrimental effect on production incentives in the rural areas. What agriculture there is in the other three desert nations is highly subsidised; and it is easy to increase these subsidies, given their governments' favourable revenue position. Appreciation is therefore viewed as a useful anti-inflation policy, especially as these economies are all open and therefore can easily import other nations' price increases.[24]

There are three major reasons, however, why the major Middle Eastern oil exporters are reluctant to let their currencies appreciate too far. First, and probably most important, the price of crude oil is still denominated in dollars as already mentioned, so any appreciation reduces the value of oil revenues in terms of the domestic currency. Second, the less populous of the oil exporters are in the process of amassing huge investment portfolios abroad, mostly in major Western financial centres, partly as a form of security for the time when oil reseervs run out. With appreciation *vis-à-vis* the Western currencies, the rate of return on these investments must inevitably fall in terms of the domestic currency of the oil-exporting nations. The same consideration also applies to foreign exchange reserves, and many of the Gulf states have already experienced heavy losses due to changing currency parities. These states lost badly in 1967 when sterling was devalued, and consequently they shifted to dollars as their major currency reserve. Since the decline of the value of the dollar after 1971, they have, unfortunately, again lost substantial sums.

The third argument against currency appreciation in the Middle East is that it can hurt infant industries if they are struggling to establish themselves in export markets. It raises the costs of their products unduly, when costs are already high, perhaps because of inexperience, the enormous price of new equipment, or short production runs.[25] Usually infant industries are producing import substitutes rather than exports, and consequently appreciation tends to lower the degree of nominal tariff protection. The degree of effective tariff protection will not necessarily be reduced, however, since, if the industry is an assembly operation, appreciation can lower input costs, thus paradoxically increasing the protective effect. It is noticeable, however, from Table 4.2 that those countries such as Egypt and Iran which have a considerable amount of industrial plant producing import substitutes have a lower rate of appreciation. Admittedly Egypt's currency position can to a large extent be explained by its foreign exchange difficulties; but the same factor does not apply to Iran as a major oil exporter.

In contrast to most other states in the Middle East, Israel and Turkey experienced serious currency depreciations over the 1969–75 period, with the Israeli pound declining in value by over 100 per cent. Israel's payments difficulties became acute after the 1973 October war, when arms purchases from abroad increased substantially, especially from the United States. At the same time, with business incomes in the West falling because of the general world recession, contributions to Israel from the world Zionist movement also slumped. Turkey was in a similar situation, as a result of embarking on an expensive operation in Cyprus during a period when remittances from its migrant workers in Europe were falling with the slump in employment in German and French manufacturing industry. Both Israel and Turkey have used high interest rate policies to support their domestic currencies, as Table 4.3 shows. This has the unfortunate side-effect, however, of making finance for domestic investment very expensive.[26] The policy is designed to attract foreign funds into Israeli pounds and Turkish lira rather than keep domestic funds within the country, as foreign exchange restrictions apply to the latter in any case. In both countries the high interest rates have not been attractive enough to bring in sufficient funds to prevent the slide of the domestic currency.

Iran's high interest rate policy is also designed to attract overseas capital, because the authorities are keen to encourage foreign companies to undertake longer-term investments. This interest rate policy is not therefore a measure of desperation, as in Israel or Turkey, bidding to attract 'hot' money flows into short-run government bills and securities. Instead the Iranians hope to attract foreign funds into joint venture projects in a bid to harness foreign expertise for local industry.[27] The Iranian authorities believe that the fruits of foreign technical assistance will be greater if parent companies have a financial stake in the local concern, rather than merely doing the work on a contract basis. These high interest rates ensure that only sound projects with a significant

TABLE 4.3. Structure of interest rates in the Middle East

	Rate (%)							Change 1969–75 (%)	Greatest variation (%)
	1969	1970	1971	1972	1973	1974	1975		
Israel	7·6	8·5	8·7	9·0	9·0	9·3	11·6	+53	53
Turkey	7·5	9·0	9·0	9·0	8·7	8·7	8·7	+16	20
Iran	8·0	8·0	7·0	7·5	9·0	9·0	8·0	0	29
Jordan	5·2	5·2	5·2	5·2	5·0	5·0	8·0	+54	60
Egypt ⎫ Syria ⎬ Libya ⎭	5·0	5·0	5·0	5·0	5·0	5·0	5·0	0	0

Source: I.M.F., *International Financial Statistics*, March 1976.

return get undertaken. There can be little doubt that if similar policies had been adopted in Egypt, Syria and Libya, many of the marginal projects undertaken would have been scrapped, which might have been a blessing, given the doubtful prospects for many of the schemes. If Egypt and Syria had used interest rate policy to defend their currencies, this at least might have been one favourable spin-off. Jordan raised interest rates in 1975 for reasons similar to Iran's, and this high interest rate policy will probably be continued there, because the price of the country's major export, phosphates, fell dramatically after October 1975. Thus a policy designed with long-term considerations in mind may well prove useful in the sort run as well, if foreigners are encouraged to hold government securities denominated in Jordanian dinars.[28]

From the analysis presented in this chapter, it is clear that tariff and exchange rates can, and have, been used as major tools of government economic policy in the Middle East. Governments have the choice of minimising or abolishing tariffs, and adopting exchange rate policies which encourage the expansion of the export sector as an engine of growth, thus developing along the lines of comparative advantage. Alternatively, they can adopt import substitution policies, as most of the governments of the more populous states of the Middle East have done in recent years, using tariffs and exchange rates to protect their new infant industries. The use of these policies in this way is, of course, a second-best means of promoting development and industrialisation, since it creates distortions in both production and consumption. A first-best solution would be to pay direct subsidies to infant industries so that they could survive international competition. The cost of these subsidies would be clearly visible for all to see. This, of course, would include domestic taxpayers, who might be reluctant to support such a policy. The tax base of most of the major Middle Eastern countries is very limited, apart from actual oil revenues, and income disparities are marked. High-income earners see it as in their own private interests to resist such proposals, which would hurt them financially, even though from the point of view of society as a whole, subsidies financed through taxation may be the first-best solution. Given that high-income earners wield enormous political power in most Middle Eastern states, however, it is not surprising that governments opt for tariffs as a soft alternative to subsidies, and an easier, politically expedient solution. What appears at first sight to be costless is nevertheless in the long-run costly economically: once market imperfections are established through a deliberate act of policy, they may be difficult to clear away. The major oil-producing nations would be well advised to consider these alternatives carefully, especially as, compared to their vast financial resources, the cost of subsidies to domestic industry is not likely to prove of major consequence. In the final two chapters some of the ramifications of Middle East tariff and exchange rate policies will be reviewed, first for intra-regional trade and then for trade with the outside world.

5 Intra-Regional Trade and Factor Mobility

At first sight there appears to be tremendous scope for trade and commerce between the nations of the Middle East because, to a large extent, they complement each other with regard to their resources. Egypt, for example, with its plentiful manpower but lack of capital, is the natural centre for the supply of labour-intensive goods such as textiles or clothing for the whole region. Saudi Arabia, because of its abundant financial resources but labour shortages, is an obvious location for capital intensive industries, especially those requiring a plentiful supply of cheap energy, although the country's technological deficiencies must first be overcome. In contrast Israel boasts a high level of technology and has a well trained workforce, but, like Egypt, has a great shortage of capital. It is therefore well suited to supply the whole region with technologically advanced goods, such as machine tools or electronic equipment. Iran, with its long craft tradition, could similarly be the main centre in the Middle East for the production of high-quality consumer products including furniture, clothing, and possibly footwear, particularly for the higher-income end of the market.[1]

This type of intra-regional specialisation would undoubtedly be econimcally advantageous, for it avoids wasteful duplication in the provision of production facilities. In the Middle East at present there are numerous instances of separate plants being developed simultaneously in several countries; yet, as might be expected, because of the limited extent of the local market, each is operated at only a low level of its potential production capacity.[2] This is the case in the iron and steel industry, for example; Saudi Arabia has ambitious plans to expand its production capacity by building a huge steel rolling mill while, at the same time in neighbouring Egypt, the Helwan steel plant is being used well below its capacity because of lack of local demand. A low level of utilisation, however, inevitably results in production being very expensive per unit of output because, with large plants of this type, fixed costs are necessarily high. When it is not economically feasible to build many small plants, owing to indivisibilities in production, as in the case of iron and steel, it would be preferable to concentrate production in the Middle East in a few large and efficient plants; in practice this means building no new plants and using to the full existing production capacity.

When countries base their industrial development strategy on the provision of large-scale capital intensive plants, as in most of the Middle East, the problem of markets looms large. In virtually all the countries of the region the domestic market is severely limited for a wide range of consumer products and for almost the entire range of intermediate and capital goods. If instead, however, production processes were geared to the wider market requirements of the Middle East as a whole, it would be possible to take advantage of economies of scale to lower production costs. This is one of the strongest arguments in support of economic co-operation in the region. Despite the fact that most of the countries in the area are deeply committed to various forms of economic planning, there has been no attempt in recent years to undertake integrated regional planning on even a limited scale. In the Gulf, for example, two large aluminium smelters are at present being built which can take advantage of local cheap energy resources.[3] Unfortunately, however, as there is already an excess supply of aluminium-smelting capacity in the world, market prospects in the West and elsewhere appear unpromising. The Middle Eastern market itself is nevertheless sufficient to justify the building of one smelter. Construction of a second smelter therefore represents a serious misuse of investment funds, with little chance of a positive return, even in terms of job creation, given the capital intensive nature of the industry.

ATTEMPTS AT ECONOMIC CO-OPERATION

In the time of the Ottoman Empire most of the Middle East region comprised one economic unit, which extended from what is now southern Yugoslavia down through the heart of the empire in Turkey to the deserts of Arabia and North Africa. The territory which since 1948 has comprised the state of Israel was in the direct path of important trade routes between the Nile Valley and Turkey, and there was a rail link connecting Cairo to Jaffa and Haifa along the Mediterranean coast through Gaza. After the break-up of the Ottoman Empire following the First World War these trade routes declined in importance because the areas to the east of the Mediterranean were split up for separate administration by the British and French victors and trade with Turkey virtually ceased. The rail link between Egypt and British-administered Palestine was maintained, however, and this link assumed a new economic importance during the years of the Second World War. At that time the allies set up the Middle East Supply Centre, which was to harness all the economic resources of the area for the war effort against the Germans and Italians, who were occupying most of north Africa.[4] Although this centre proved to be a great success in providing food for the allied troops taking part in the desert campaigns, following the war the sense of urgency disappeared and the idea of the centre was abandoned. This was to be the last time the use of Middle Eastern resources was planned on an integrated regional basis.

Following Israel's emergence as a state in 1948, and the conflict of that year, an economic boycott was announced by the Arab states, and all trade links with Israel were broken. There were no capital transfers between the new Israeli state and its Arab neighbours, although there was limited labour mobility, with some of the Arabs remaining in Israel being allowed to travel to neighbouring Arab states. Nevertheless, the economic isolation of Israel in the region was almost total, a situation that was to prove detrimental to all parties from the economic point of view. Not only was trade between Israel and its Arab neighbours halted, but intra-Arab trade also suffered owing to the closure of trade routes through Israel. Goods going from Egypt to Lebanon or Syria went by sea instead of land, which hindered communications. This factor contributed to the fall of the short-lived union between Egypt and Syria.[5] Jordan was the country most affected by the blockade of trade routes, because its exports and imports either had to go via Aqaba on the Red Sea, which is really only suitable for trade with the East, or else had to go overland by Damascus to the congested port of Beirut for shipping.

At the time the Arab Common Market was set up in 1964, the volume of trade between Middle Eastern states represented less than one-twentieth of the area's total trade. The founders of this common market hoped that its formation would help to reverse the decline in intra-Middle East trade and reduce the area's dependence on the outside world. Most of the countries of the area were highly specialised in the production of one or two export commodities, and were very vulnerable to fluctuations in world market conditions. It was hoped that intra-Middle East trade would reduce this dependence through diversifying trade, and therefore help to reverse the adverse trends that were visible in the terms of trade of most countries of the region. In practice, however, the Arab Common Market only existed on paper for the first 9 years following the signing of the treaty.[6] The proportion of intra-Middle East trade relative to trade with the outside world remains at a very low level, even though it showed some increase over the 1965–69 period cited in Table 5.1.

TABLE 5.1. Share of Intra-Arab Common Market (A.C.M.) trade in the total trade of the A.C.M. countries

| | Exports (%) | | Imports (%) | |
	1965	1969	1965	1969
Jordan	24·5	61·2	8·1	11·3
Iraq	14·1	44·0	7·8	10·3
Syria	6·7	14·4	11·1	8·8
Egypt	2·9	4·2	3·2	3·6
Sudan	5·0	5·1	4·0	4·7
Kuwait	10·8	16·8	3·2	4·1
Total	5·7	9·2	4·1	5·6

Source: 'Foreign Trade of the Countries of the Council of Arab Economic Unity and of the Arab Common Market including possibilities for Increasing Intra Trade', report of the *United Nations Economic and Social Office*, Beirut, 1971. Data from statistical tables presented in part 5 of the report.

It is apparent that Jordan is the country which trades most with other Arab countries, followed by Iraq, which has rapidly been increasing its share of intra-regional trade in recent years. Both these countries run large trade surpluses with their Arab trading partners as does Kuwait. Most of the large trade surplus of Iraq and Kuwait is, however, accounted for by one product—oil. This represents the main intra-regional export for both these states, as well as being of course their main export to the world at large. The trade patterns illustrated in Table 5.1 may to some extent be explained by the communications factor already mentioned. Intra-regional trade is much greater amongst the Asian countries of the market, which have contiguous land frontiers; but there is little trade between these countries and Egypt or the Sudan, since overland trade links are broken by the Israeli presence. A further factor which played an increasing part in explaining the changing patterns of intra-regional trade was the growth of export credits. The positions of intra-regional exports and imports were reversed during the 1960s in relation to the total value of trade. In 1960 intra-regional imports accounted for almost 8 per cent of the area's total imports, but by 1969 this had declined to 5·6 per cent. Meanwhile intra-area exports rose from 5 per cent in 1960 to over 9 per cent in 1969 within the Arab Common Market. The oil-exporting countries such as Kuwait and Iraq did not demand immediate payment from the region's oil-importing states, which include Syria, Sudan and Jordan. The latter is nevertheless in a more fortunate position because it is an increasingly significan exporter of phosphates while, in addition, it is one of the main sources of agricultural produce for the Gulf and consequently has little difficulty in paying for its oil imports.

From the start, however, the Arab Common Market was not a viable proposition, despite this trade. There are several factors which help explain why it did so little to foster Middle East trade.[7] First, it was restricted to Muslim countries and not only excluded Israel, as might be expected, but also Lebanon, whose Christians did not want to be part of any wider Muslim community of nations.[8] Trade is negligible between the Arab and non-Arab states in the region. The persistent hostilities between Iraq and Iran has resulted in few trade links being developed between these two countries, even though trade could bring substantial mutual benefits. Admittedly, both countries are to some extent trying to develop a range of infant industries which overlap, so therefore neither would welcome the competition which trade would bring. The range of industry in Iran is wider, however, and includes, for example, plants for vehicle assembly, which are not found in Iraq. In return for providing Iran with an additional market outlet, Iraqi firms could be licensed to produce a range of components for Iranian vehicles. Similar arrangements could be negotiated between Turkey and its Arab neighbours. The historical experience of the Arab states of Ottoman domination has made them reluctant to consider taking measures to promote trade with Turkey right up to the present time. It is perhaps ironic that, at the same time, all the countries of the eastern Mediterranean, including Turkey, the Arab states, and Israel, are separately trying to promote trade with the European Economic Community but are doing little to encourage trade with each other.[9] Today the countries of the Middle East have undoubtedly more to lose from concluding unequal trade agreements with the E.E.C., than from economic domination by their neighbours. The political conflicts of the Middle East have an enormous cost in terms of the waste of economic opportunities.

Apart from these political difficulties, several other factors have served to hinder the growth of intra-Middle East trade. First, although the Arab Common Market Agreement of 1964 provided for free trade in industrial products, countries were allowed to submit lists of goods which they wanted to be excluded. Admittedly, the Kuwaitis only put one item on their list; but the Jordanians originally wanted 77 goods excluded, while Syria asked for 71 exceptions, Egypt 52 and Iraq 35. The Economic Unity Council, which had been set up to enforce the rules of the Arab Common Market expressed serious reservations about the length of these lists, but nevertheless approved them without revision.

A second major factor which prevented the Arab Common Market fostering a growing volume of intra-Middle East trade was the war of 1967, which came only 3 years after the signing of the customs union agreement. Owing to the war, the reduction of tariffs amongst the member states of the Arab Common Market was delayed, and it was only by 1973 that tariffs came to be abolished for the limited range of industrial goods, 4 years later than anticipated. Intra-Middle East trade has not responded to these tariff cuts to any great extent, however, probably because quotas and exchange controls played a more significant role in restricting trade than tariffs in any case, and these quantitative restrictions continue to apply.[10] In addition there is little incentive for consumers in areas like the Gulf to purchase industrial goods such as cars from Egypt, when they can import the same goods, better produced, from the West. In the rich Gulf market the demand for consumer durables may be relatively price inelastic, so even if the reduction in tariffs did give Egyptian products a price advantage, their goods may still not sell. The low tariff rates prevailing in the Gulf reduce any chance of trade diversion, with Middle East supplies being substituted for European or American imports. It seems likely that, in so far as the Common Market does work, trade diversion is probably more significant than trade creation anyway, so welfare is not necessarily improved for the Middle East countries. This factor alone limits the usefulness of the market, as the inefficiencies prevailing in production centres like Egypt mean that it may take years for their infant industries to reap the advantages of economies of scale associated with a larger market. Thus when the standard Vinerian customs union analysis is applied to the Arab Common Market, the conclusion must be that the detrimental effects will exceed any possible benefits, even if a relatively long time horizon is adopted.[11]

Few of the dynamic benefits of intra-regional trade are in fact applicable in the Middle East. One of the main dynamic arguments for regional integration is that the increased competition of the wider market will force industries to be more efficient. Few governments in the Middle East are going to stand by and watch some of their carefully fostered infant industries put out of business by foreign competition, even if its source is within the region. There is too limited a range of job opportunities in each country for workers to be easily redeployed from the industry contracting under competition to alternative employment. Thus proposals for co-operation to avoid wasteful duplication in the future have more chance of receiving a favourable response from the countries concerned, despite the past record already mentioned, than arguments in favour of a freely competitive environment.

SCOPE FOR LABOUR MOBILITY

Historically there has been considerable movement of peoples in the Middle East. Most major migrations in recent years have been within the region, apart from the continuing immigration into Israel from western Europe, North America and, increasingly, the Soviet Union. Much of the immigration of Jews into Israel at the time of the country's independence was from other areas of the Middle East, however, including Egypt and Iraq, though some came from every Arab state.[12] At the same time there was an outflow of Muslim and Christian Palestinians into neighbouring Arab states, especially Jordan and Lebanon.[13] In some respects a swap of population can be considered to have taken place, and many of the people involved share remarkably similar backgrounds. This factor undoubtedly helps the different religions and cultural groups involved to understand each others' aspirations and problems, even if there is at the same time considerable mistrust and antagonism which has built up over the years.

In recent years the major migrations within the Middle East have been in response to economic rather than political factors, although many of the people who have been involved, especially the Palestinians, were originally displaced for political reasons. Essentially the migrations have involved a transfer of labour, from labour abundant states such as Egypt or Lebanon, to states with rich financial resources, such as the oil-rich producers of the Gulf. Such a transfer makes sound economic sense, since labour, especially skilled manpower, is in very short supply in Saudi Arabia, the Gulf sheikdoms and Libya. These desert states were able to support only very small populations prior to the oil boom; yet now they all want to develop modern diversified economies. The local population, who were largely nomadic tribesmen, were unable, and often unwilling, to work for the oil companies, even when high wages were offered. Therefore other Arabs, mostly Egyptians and Palestinians, took their place. These Arab migrants not only provided the manpower needed by the oil sector, but also worked in government and carried out the services which the new states required. Their impact has been enormous, as in Kuwait for example, where most of the workforce are non-Kuwaitis, and more than half of the country's total population are immigrants.

This massive inflow of immigrants may have been economically beneficial, but it has inevitably created social tensions. Although the newcomers were welcomed in the Gulf in the early years because they filled an essential gap, as the local inhabitants became more conscious of their position and power, resentments began to grow. Measures have therefore been introduced to curb immigration, including that from other Arab countries, despite the fact that the countries involved are all members of the Arab Common Market. Yet the first provision of the Economic Unity Agreement signed in 1964, and subsequently ratified by Kuwait amongst others, was that there should be freedom of movement of labour, as well as 'freedom of residence, work, employment, and exercise of economic activity'.[14] In spite of their immense wealth, the governments of the Gulf states have not extended the generous welfare benefits enjoyed by their own citizens to cover migrant workers or their families. Many of the Arab immigrants in Kuwait live in poor conditions and receive only limited incomes, but they still have to pay for their children's education and bear hospital expenses themselves. In contrast, within the European Common Market, migrant workers from member states can enjoy the full welfare benefits of any host country in which they choose to take up employment.

The most welcome immigrants are, not surprisingly, those with special skills to offer. When such highly trained people migrate, what in effect takes place is a kind of technological transfer. For the host countries there is a substantial element of subsidy in such migration because they derive the benefits of the training the migrants have received without having to pay the costs themselves. In the Middle East these subsidies on education or human capital have gone to those states which are already well endowed with financial resources rather than the region's poor states. Many of the Palestinians receiving education which has been paid for by the United Nations Relief and Welfare Agency, (U.N.R.W.A.), designed to help the refugees, have migrated to the oil-rich states in the Gulf, attracted by the promise of high salaries. The Palestinians remaining in the refugee camps tend to be those least able to take care of themselves. Despite almost three decades of U.N.R.W.A. education scholarships, there is still a shortage of doctors and well-qualified teachers in the Palestinian refugee camps. Similarly, the most highly qualified Egyptians are often found living outside Egypt, and many are working under contract in the Gulf and Libya. Yet in Egyptian villages there is still a great shortage of health personnel, and the country's state-run industries find it difficult to keep able accountants and competent managerial staff. This kind of technological transfer therefore amounts to a brain-drain, which helps those countries which could easily help themselves in any case; paradoxically, the nations which have sacrificed most to build up their technological skills suffer most.[15]

It is customary now in the field of development economics to regard technology as a separate factor of production. A considerable amount of literature has grown up on the subject of technological transfer, but most of this is concerned with the problem of international transfers from developed to less-developed countries,[16] rather than transfers within regions of the Third World. Less-developed countries have often ended up importing inappropriate technology, and there are many instances of this in the Middle East. For example, during the last 20 years, several countries, including Egypt and Syria, have undertaken major industrial expansions based on capital intensive production techniques. Yet their resource endowments of abundant manpower but insufficient capital indicate that the adoption of more labour intensive processes would have been appropriate, perhaps based on intermediate technology. These policies have only accentuated dualistic tendencies within the major Arab economies, with the modern industrial sector employing small numbers of highly paid elite workers, but absorbing most of the investment resources, while agriculture stagnates owing to insufficient finance. All this is a familiar story to economic observers of the Third World. In the Middle East, however, the economic consequences of the misallocation of resources have been increased by the fact that resources for civilian projects were so limited in the first place, as so much was channelled off for military purposes.

If, instead of relying on external technical assistance, the Middle East countries co-operated more with each other, many of the pitfalls associated with advanced technology could be avoided. Resources could be pooled in order to finance research and development of intermediate technology more suited to the factor endowment of the region. It is, after all, the people from the Middle East themselves who have the greatest understanding of their own region and are therefore best able to judge whether a particular technique of production is suitable. They can judge how employees will respond to the introduction of a new system of work. In addition there are fewer communications problems with technical assistance when local people are involved, as foreign experts often have no knowledge of the language and little sympathy with local customs. Even if the technical assistants working in the Arab states were Iranian or Turkish, or vice versa, they would still have a major advantage over their Western counterparts in these respects.

In the event of a lasting peace settlement in the Middle East, Israelis could also play a major role in the field of technical assistance. Israel has already gained considerable experience through giving assistance to projects in Africa, Asia and Latin America, and there have been some limited schemes for co-operation with Iran.[17] The mere fact that Israel is a Middle Eastern state, and therefore an insider, means the country can provide the right kind of technical assistance, especially in fields such as agricultural development. Many Israelis, as already pointed out, came from the Arab states themselves and can not only speak Arabic, but are accustomed to dealing with their Arab neighbours. Since 1967 there has been increased working contact between Jews and Arabs, as the West Bank and Gaza have been more closely integrated into the economy of Israel.[18] There would seem to be tremendous scope for technical co-operation and perhaps, if co-operation in this field was economically successful, it could pave the way for greater mutual trust and understanding throughout the Middle East.

CAPITAL TRANSFERS

Given the constraints operating at present on labour mobility and even technical assistance, the potential for capital transfers would appear greater, at least at first sight. These factor movements, of course, to a large extent complement each other and cannot be looked upon merely as substitutes. Nevertheless, economists interested in issues of regional policy often argue that it is better to take work to the workers, rather than rely on labour migration.[19] A high degree of capital mobility can soon iron out regional resource imbalances, and this may be easier to achieve, yet have fewer consequent costs, than labour mobility. When labour is moved on a permanent basis there are the costs of housing, as well as the expenses incurred in providing all the other necessary services including health, education and social amenities. These costs, admittedly, may not be as great in the Middle East as in the West, owing to the lower living standards and expectations generally prevailing, but nevertheless costs can mount up. In the Gulf, for instance, where the immigrants mostly pay for the welfare services they use, there are still opportunity costs in terms of the scarce resources used, and the cost of these services is increased for everyone else, whether as private consumers or as taxpayers.

The financing of new investment needed to expand employment opportunities in the Middle East in industry does not present difficulties.[20] Even before the petroleum price rises of the winter 1973–74, several major oil producers including Saudi Arabia and Kuwait had substantial surplus funds. In Saudi Arabia, for example, the population is estimated at between 4 and 9 million, but in 1974 oil revenues exceeded $26,000 million, representing around $6500 per capita if the minimum estimate is taken, or over $2800 if the higher figure is accepted. Yet in desert states such as Saudi Arabia the absorptive capacity is limited, and much of the money in the past has inevitably been recycled back to the West, with minimal local multiplier effects. Most revenue accrues to the royal household, who have been conspicuous consumers of Western goods. Much has been, and is being, used for the purchase of military equipment, which will do little to foster development. The funds invested locally through Petromin to encourage industrial diversification outside the petroleum sector must inevitably lose money because of the absence of markets and skilled local labour to run the installations. Although it is often asserted that Saudi Arabia has little trouble spending its oil revenues, much of the expenditure has been unproductive and from the development point of view has represented a serious misuse of funds. The Saudi Arabians themselves stand to lose out in the long run if their oil revenues continue to be spent as they have been, since they will have no long-term security or income to fall back on when the oil eventually runs out.

Intra-Middle East financial transfers account for only a small proportion of the capital movements which occur between the region and the outside world. On balance the Middle East runs a substantial deficit because the large outflows from the oil-rich states greatly exceed the aid and capital inflows from the West and the Communist bloc. Most of the aid from the Communist world to countries such as Egypt, Syria and Iraq has been to finance the purchase of military equipment, and much of this has been in the form of loans rather than grants. Thus Egypt's indebtedness to the Soviet Union alone amounts to a staggering £5000 million according to a recent estimate.[21]

The rich oil-producing nations have been reluctant, however, to make finance available to the poorer nations of the Middle East, even those with serious debt problems. Most of the surplus oil funds from Saudi Arabia, for example, which could not be absorbed locally, have been placed in short-term bank deposits in Western financial centres. The Saudis have little investment experience, and are reluctant to commit sums for longer periods anywhere. Although a small Development Fund has been set up to help poorer Muslim countries, the finance provided amounts to only a minute proportion of the funds going to the West.[22] Larger amounts have been offered to Egypt for the purchase of Western military equipment, but this will hardly do much to help develop the Nile Valley.

Kuwaiti investors have acquired much more experience in handling large-scale finance. They have also been reluctant, however, to promote projects in the Middle East, where there are very uncertain markets and where the threat of nationalisation is ever-present. Most investment has therefore been channelled into Western stock markets, either directly or through the Beirut banking system. In addition, large amounts have been invested in property in Europe and the United States, as this is believed to be the most secure of assets. The amounts of money allocated to the Kuwait Fund for Arab Economic Development are very limited when contrasted with these enormous amounts being invested in the West. Nevertheless the fund has played a useful role in the Middle East, and it could perhaps be regarded as a model for any future institutions set up to channel Middle East oil revenues into investment projects within the region rather than outside it.[23]

The Kuwait Fund is run on the same lines as the World Bank. It provides loans, usually at interest rates well below commercial levels, on a long-term basis to aid particular projects. Arab countries who wish to borrow from the Fund submit their proposals, and then the Fund sends out its technical experts to consider whether the projects put forward are viable.[24] Major loans made include one of almost 5 million Kuwaiti Dinars to Jordan to help irrigation projects on the Zarqa River, with the repayment period set at 25 years, and interest at only 3 per cent. Over one-quarter of all loans made by the Fund are to support agricultural projects, although Iraq borrowed 3·8 million Kuwaiti Dinars to finance its expansion of cement production. The interest charges on this loan were 4 per cent per annum, and the repayment period agreed was 13 years with a 2-year initial grace period. The interest charges on loans for agricultural development are more generous than for other purposes, and the grace period longer, as Table 5.2 illustrates. Even for loans for infrastructure, or industrial development, there is a large element of subsidy, however. This aid component can be estimated by working out the difference between the concessionary interest terms offered and commercial rates, and adding in the grace period. Viewed in this way, over 50 per cent of the lending for industrial projects can be regarded as aid, and a correspondingly larger proportion for infrastructure and agriculture. The relative lack of alternative profitable investment projects in the West, and the prevailing uncertainty over exchange rates, has to some extent lowered the opportunity costs of lending within the Middle East region, however. Recently the Fund has been making funds available at 4·5–5 per cent for industrial projects where the potential for profit was considered to be high. The gap between the Fund's lending rate and commercial rates seems to be narrowing.[25]

TABLE 5.2. Terms of loans granted by the Kuwait Fund for Arab Economic Development

Projects	Interest rates	Payments period	Grace period
Agriculture	3%	23 years	4½ years
Other infrastructure	4%	15 years	3–4 years
Industry	4%	13 years	2½ years

Source: Kuwait Fund For Arab Economic Development, *Annual Report* 1974–75.

The Kuwait Government's original motivation in establishing the Fund back in 1962 was political: they hoped to win recognition for their newly independent state from all the countries represented in the Arab league and, in this way, counter Iraqi territorial claims on their valuable oil deposits. This aim has now been achieved, and the operation of the Kuwait Fund admittedly helped to ensure this successful political outcome at a fairly modest price. Despite this political motivation behind the lending, the Fund does, nevertheless, adopt proper techniques for project appraisal when making a loan, as already mentioned. After all, if a project proves in practice not to be viable and, as a consequence, the borrower cannot repay, this may be politically counterproductive, as debtors in this position seldom like their creditors. The Fund lends to a wide spectrum of countries of varying political persuasions, as can be seen from Table 5.3. This shows that Egypt has been the largest single beneficiary, although Sudan has also been receiving a large share

TABLE 5.3. Distribution of loans by the Kuwait Fund for Arab Economic Development

Country	Agriculture	Transport and storage	Electricity	Industry	Total	% *
					(million KD)	
Jordan	6·48	—	3·26	4·48	14·22	8·83
Bahrain	—	0·50	7·35	1·49	9·34	5·80
Tunisia	5·20	3·75	8·35	2·00	19·30	11·98
Algeria	—	10·00	—	—	10·00	6·21
Sudan	9·11	7·00	—	6·17	22·28	13·83
Syria	—	7·00	9·90	2·00	18·90	11·73
Iraq	—	—	2·62	3·76	6·38	3·96
Lebanon	—	0·80	1·66	—	2·46	1·52
Egypt	—	27·80	—	7·00	34·80	21·61
Morocco	10·05	—	—	3·25	13·30	8·26
South Yemen	4·53	—	—	·—	4·53	2·81
North Yemen	2·22	0·28	—	3·00	5·50	3·41
Total	37·59	57·13	33·14	33·15	161·00	100·00
% *	23·34	35·48	20·58	20·58	100·00	

Note: * Does not add up to 100 because of rounding.
Source: Kuwait Fund for Arab Economic Development, *Annual Report*, 1974–75.

of the Fund's total lending. None of the other countries, apart from Tunisia and Syria, have received more than one-tenth of the total funds disbursed. The number of countries receiving assistance has gradually been increasing, and the Fund has recently, despite its name, started lending to states outside the Arab world, even including non-Muslim states such as India. To some extent this reflects Kuwait's new affluence following the 1974 oil price increases. However, it may also be the consequence of a desire to repair the damage caused to Third World countries by the petroleum price rises, although in the process the Kuwaitis, and especially those Palestinians resident there, may also hope to win additional political allies for the Arab cause against Israel.

The amount of capital which the Kuwait Government has made available to the Fund has increased twentyfold since the organisation was established. The largest increase in the Fund's statutory capital was in July 1974, when it increased from just over $700 million to over $3400 million. At the same time, however, Kuwait's prime minister was appointed to the Fund's Board of Directors, which reflects the government's concern that there should be increasing political accountability, given the increased magnitude of the financial sums involved. Total loan disbursements still fall well short of the statutory capital, even though they have increased in value to over $547·4 million in 1974. The total amount of capital actually paid into the Fund is only equivalent at present to one-third of the statutory capital. Even this, however, is well in excess of the loan commitments made by the Fund. An examination of the balance sheets actually reveals that the Fund's lending for development projects is less than the residual amounts held in the form of commercial assets and government securities. Most of these investments are in fact in major Western financial centres, which belies the original intention of the Fund to use its resources to promote regional development in the Middle East.

Apart from the Kuwait Fund, there are two similar, but more recently established, organisations which perform a similar role in recycling capital from the oil-rich economies to those in the Middle East in need of financial assistance. The first of these, the Abu Dhabi Fund for Economic Development, is just starting operations and is being organised on the same lines as the Kuwait Fund, but it has less capital at its disposal. The second organisation, the Arab Fund for Economic and Social Development (A.F.E.S.D.) plays a much wider role.[26] Its charter was approved by the Arab Economic Council in 1968, but it only started operations in 1972. This fund is to finance development projects in the entire Arab region, since the Arab Economic Council represents all the

Arab countries, unlike the Economic Unity Council mentioned earlier which is primarily concerned with the members of the Arab Common Market. The initial authorised capital of A.F.E.S.D. was only $340 million, much less than the amount of capital which the Kuwait Fund had at its disposal in 1972. Unlike the Kuwait Fund, however, A.F.E.S.D. loans have been used to finance projects of a social rather than economic nature, where investment returns cannot be easily quantified. Aid is therefore being given to provide better health facilities, as well as education and housing. A.F.E.S.D. also differs from the Kuwait Fund because of its multinational nature; its finance comes from all the major oil-producing Arab countries and not merely one state. Rather than granting loans on a bilateral basis like the Kuwait Fund, A.F.E.S.D. favours regional schemes involving more than one country in a project, especially those in frontier areas which tend to be neglected.

In addition to these government-financed agencies which aid the poorer states of the Middle East, a further organisation, the Inter-Arab Investment Guarantee Corporation, has been set up to encourage private investors to keep their money within the region by financing industrial expansion.[27] The corporation provides an insurance service for businessmen investing in stocks or bonds in the 11 Arab states which have ratified the agreement under which the organisation was created. It also covers funds invested in the take-over of local firms, finance used to establish subsidiaries, and private loans made for periods of longer than 3 years. The greatest fear of businessmen undertaking these kinds of ventures in the Middle East is that their assets will be expropriated through nationalisation and that they will not be adequately compensated. Despite the fact that the corporation cannot guarantee assets against seizure, they at least provide an insurance cover, although this is only up to the value of the subscription made by each participating country, for investors from that country. Originally the amount insured in respect of investments was to be up to twice the subscription made by a participating country. As presently constituted, there seems little advantage to be gained from the multinational nature of the scheme with regard to insurance cover. Each state might as well provide its own cover for its investors. The total capital of the corporation is only $34 million in any case, which is far from adequate given the service the founders of the corporation envisaged it would provide. In the event of a seizure of foreign-owned assets in a major country participating in the scheme, such as Egypt or Syria, these funds would certainly not be enough to provide the compensation which the corporation agrees to pay to investors. The best hedge against risk for private investors placing funds in the Middle East is to spread their assets over as large a range of countries as possible.[28]

There has been a conspicuous lack of any measures designed to promote intra-regional capital transfers between the Arab and non-Arab countries of the Middle East. Although the Kuwait Fund now lends to non-Arab states, these have been located outside the region entirely, apart from Afghanistan which can scarcely be considered a Middle East state. No funds have been advanced to finance projects in Turkey, despite the fact that the country has enormous investment potential, yet a great shortage of capital. Turkey can boast a larger pool of skilled labour on which to draw than any other country in the Middle East, as large numbers of Turks have gained industrial experience in West Germany and elsewhere in Europe as migrant labourers. In contrast to the lack of collaboration between the so-called northern tier countries of the Middle East, Iran and Turkey, and their Arab neighbours to the south, there has been at least some limited economic co-operation between the non-Arab states themselves. An agency for Regional Co-operation for Development (R.C.D.) was set up in 1964 between Iran, Pakistan and Turkey. The motivation behind the establishment of this agency was largely political, as there was strong encouragement from the United States. It was hoped that by strengthening the economies of these front-line states bordering the Soviet Union, the populations would offer greater resistance to communist infiltration. The R.C.D. was to some extent viewed as the economic arm of the Central Asian Treaty Organisation, (CENTO) the defence alliance that linked the states militarily. However, by the time the R.C.D. started work in 1968, Iran and Turkey had already improved their relations with the Soviet Union, while Pakistan was seeking Chinese support for its continuing conflict with India and her Russian backers. The attempt at regional economic planning of investment was therefore rather half-hearted, and the only concrete achievement of the co-operation seems to have been the construction of one aluminium smelter. Some other joint investment projects were sponsored through the R.C.D. programme, but they were in border areas and would probably have taken place anyway.[29]

Despite the enormous gains that greater intra-regional trade and factor mobility could bring to the Middle East, this account illustrates how those attempts at economic co-operation within both the Arab and the northern tier states have achieved little to date. While the political obstacles to co-operation remain, the probability of the successful expansion of trade in the context of a common market is slender; and there is only limited prospect of extending the common market to include factors of production such as labour, technology or capital. In reality the Arab Common Market can scarcely be considered as a customs union, given the quota restrictions and lack of currency convertibility amongst the member states. The R.C.D., in practice, does not even constitute a free trade area. For the foreseeable future it seems certain that the trade relations of the Middle East will continue to be orientated towards the outside world rather than intra-regionally.

6 The Middle East and the International Economy

During the 1970s the Middle East has experienced a trade boom and has become the world's fastest growing import market. The recent world recession, which was largely caused by the oil price rises of 1974, ironically only marginally affected the Middle East, which was the one region of the world where business was brisker than ever before. Of course, to a large extent it was in fact the rise in oil revenues that created the boom conditions, and this more than offset the reductions in the volume of oil output caused by the recession in demand in the industrialised world. Despite the tremendous increase in revenue, it is perhaps strange that trade has nevertheless grown so much, given the desire of most of the countries involved to become less dependent on economic links with the outside world and given the widespread encouragement of diversification through import substitution. This trade growth was not surprising, however, since, with the vast increase in oil revenues, the recipient countries were naturally keen to embark upon ambitious development plans. These inevitably entailed a huge increase in imports because domestic substitutes were not available.[1] Most governments believed that this strategy would be preferable in the long term, because eventually, as domestic production capacity increased, dependence would lessen. The only alternative was to hold the oil revenues either in some form of international paper assets, such as Special Drawing Rights, government bills issued by the oil-consuming nations, or else in private investments in Western markets. This would only increase the oil exporters' economic dependence in the long term and leave them in a vulnerable position as *rentier* states once the oil revenues ran out, for they would be left holding paper assets rather than a material resource. Given this choice, it was to be expected that the Middle East oil producers would import up to the limit of the handling capacity of their ports and transportation systems.

GROWTH OF EXPORT TRADE

Over 90 per cent of the export trade of the Middle East is accounted for by one commodity—oil. Consequently Saudi Arabia is the region's largest single exporter in terms of the value of foreign exchange earnings, as Table 6.1 shows, while Iran is second. The earnings of both countries increased dramatically to over three times their previous annual level in one year, 1974. Kuwait, Libya and Iraq, the next largest oil producers, experienced similar increases in export revenues because of the enormous increase in oil prices following the October 1973 war with Israel.[2] This rise in export revenues only served to accentuate the gap between the oil exporters and non-oil exporters of the Middle East. Countries such as Egypt and Sudan, which still rely heavily on one agricultural commodity—cotton—for their export proceeds, experienced a decline in the earnings over the 1973–75 period; and the drop was quite marked when measured in real rather than money terms. Israel has been in a much better position, as it managed to increase its sales of citrus produce abroad, partly through widening its market outlets. In addition it tried to diversify its citrus exports, and it now exports a greater proportion of grapefruit and lemons in relation to oranges. Some of this increased fruit production comes from Gaza, which now accounts for almost 10 per cent of Israeli agricultural exports.[3] Exports of fruit juices and canned fruit have increased very rapidly in recent years and, consequently, the country has increased the value it adds locally in respect to agricultural produce.

Jordan's foreign exchanged earnings improved remarkably in 1974 due to an unprecedented rise in the world price of phosphates, the country's main export. The following year, the world's major exporters of phosphates, including Jordan, were taken by surprise when the market suddenly collapsed and the price consequently was cut back dramatically. To a large extent this downturn was a direct result of the high prices of the previous year; demand for phosphate fertilisers slumped and farmers started using substitutes, including organic material, to boost crop yields. The objective of Jordan's new 5-year plan is to increase exports of phosphates to the value of £175 million by 1980; but this target may be over-optimistic if the United States and the Soviet Union continue to increase phosphate production as they did in 1974. Nevertheless, if Jordan succeeds in diversifying its mineral exports, the planned export revenue target may not be so unrealistic. Provision is made in the country's 5-year plan for investment worth more than £45 million on potash extraction from brine and rock in the Dead Sea area. The

TABLE 6.1. Growth of exports from the Middle East (values in millions of U.S. dollars)

Country	1968	1969	1970	1971	1972	1973	1974	1975
Saudi Arabia	2026	2001	2423	3845	5490	9093	35,654	29,602
Iran	1881	2100	2623	3824	4763	6998	24,001	22,448
Kuwait	1437	1540	1901	2573	3056	3819	10,961	8510
Iraq	1041	1042	1100	1530	1369	2410	8288	N/A
Libya	1876	2167	2366	2695	2938	3995	8261	4397
Israel	602	689	734	915	1100	1389	1734	1826
Turkey	496	537	588	677	885	1317	1532	1401
Egypt	622	745	762	789	825	1117	1516	1116
Syria	172	207	203	207	287	351	784	N/A
Lebanon	146	170	198	256	350	589	N/A	N/A
Sudan	233	248	293	331	360	434	350	301
South Yemen	110	144	146	106	108	113	203	N/A
Jordan	40	41	34	32	48	58	155	N/A
North Yemen	N/A	4	3	4	4	8	13	N/A

Source: *U.N. Monthly Bulletin of Statistics*, April 1976.

United States Agency for International Development has already made a £3 million loan available on generous terms to carry out preliminary work in the El Lisan peninsula on the East Bank. This peninsula, however, lies less than 5 miles from the Israeli-occupied West Bank, so like most of Jordan's other development projects, the scheme will only be possible if there is continued peace with Israel.[4]

Lebanon's exports have been very badly affected by its internal conflict between the Christian and Muslim communities. No export figures have in fact been released for the last 2 years as a consequence of the conflict; they would probably have weakened the position of the Lebanese pound still further. It seems likely, however, that the level in 1975 was well below even the amount of 5 years ago and probably did not exceed $200 million. This is unfortunate, as the country's export performance was extremely good in 1973, partly because of a good citrus harvest, but also because of increasing exports of consumer goods to neighbouring Arab states. Lebanon's invisible exports have also been adversely affected by the conflict, although these are not included in the data given in Table 6.1 which refers only to visible earnings. Invisibles such as banking and insurance were especially important for the Lebanese economy, but it will be a long time before faith is restored in Beirut as a financial centre.

In recent years Turkey has been exporting an increasingly diverse range of goods, and the country's dependence on primary commodities such as cotton and tobacco is lessening. Turkey is growing in importance as a supplier of manufactured goods, especially textiles and other consumer items. The country sends most of its exports to western Europe, as it has an association agreement with the E.E.C., but this makes it very vulnerable to changes in market conditions there. In 1975 for instance, because of the recession in western Europe, Turkish exports fell, ending the steadily improving performance which had been experienced for almost a decade. Given the size of its population, the level of Turkish exports on a per capita basis remains low and it perhaps best compared to the level of Egypt's exports.[5] Both countries have been trying to lessen their dependence on trade through adopting import substitution policies in recent years. The Egyptians can probably learn from Turkey's experience in trying to diversify export activity, however, as they embark on an 'Open Door' policy, which hopes to encourage the establishment of export-orientated manufacturing plants in the Suez Canal area.

Syria's exports more than doubled in value in 1974 despite the setback the country experienced in the October 1973 war with Israel when several major industrial plants were destroyed. These were catering largely for the domestic market, however, as agricultural produce such as wool, cotton and cereals still constitute the country's main exports. The major factor which accounts for Syria's recent favourable export performance is the boom conditions prevailing in the markets of the country's main trading partners within the Middle East. Exports of agricultural produce to oil-exporting nations including Saudi Arabia, Iraq, and the Gulf States have increased remarkably. Road links have recently been improved with Saudi Arabia via Jordan, and Syria is co-sponsoring a feasibility study for the reconstruction of the Hijaz railway which should help to speed up export deliveries. This railway connecting Damascus to Medina was originally destroyed by Lawrence of Arabia, in the onslaught against the Turks in the First World War, and has never been rebuilt. Apart from this flourishing trade in visible exports, Syrian exports of invisibles have also been increasing in recent years, although there is little chance of Damascus replacing Beirut as a commercial centre for the region. The austere socialist regime in Damascus prompts bankers and businessmen to look elsewhere, mainly to Amman and the cities of the Gulf.

Like Syria, both North and South Yemen have improved their export performance in the Middle East because of the buoyant state of local markets. North Yemen's exports of agricultural produce, including meat, to Saudi Arabia have steadily increased, and the country has also gained substantial foreign exchange through remittances from migrant workers employed in Jiddah, Medina, and even Riyadh.[6] A large proportion of the manual workers in these cities are Yemenis, and they probably constitute a majority of those in unskilled employment in Jiddah. Through its visible exports and this invisible item, petroleum revenues have managed to trickle down into non-oil states such as North Yemen, and regional multiplier effects are undoubtedly strengthening. North Yemen has also benefited in recent years from the high price prevailing in world markets for coffee, its principal export. No figure for export proceeds for 1975 is yet available, but it seems likely that earnings will be well above the level registered in the previous year.

The trend in export prices has generally been favourable during the 1970s for most of the major trading nations of the Middle East as Table 6.2 shows. Petroleum exporters have of course experienced the most dramatic upward price changes, as the data given for Iranian petroleum exports illustrates. These prices are presented in money terms, however, denominated in the local currency of each exporting country, so the increase in real terms is not therefore so impressive. In

TABLE 6.2. Export prices in selected Middle East economies

Country	Remarks	1969	1970	1971	1972	1973	1974
Iran	Petroleum only	100	100	122	138	186	660
	Excluding petroleum	95	100	103	117	158	183
Israel	Prices in U.S.$	101	100	104	112	141	164
Turkey	General index	85	100	131	145	185	N/A
Egypt	Cotton	103	100	101	106	130	227
Syria	Cotton	101	100	108	118	123	155
	Wool	100	100	116	145	237	293
	Barley	55	100	128	86	166	162
Sudan	Cotton	118	100	84	102	143	214
Jordan	Phosphates	113	100	101	102	109	367
	Tomatoes	141	100	76	92	82	103

Note: Base 1970 = 100.
Source: I.M.F., *International Financial Statistics*, April 1976.

fact during the 1969–72 period, the real value of petroleum exports was declining in terms of the amount of imports from the industrialised world the Middle Eastern states could purchase.[7] Figures are not presented for the export prices which prevailed in the other oil-exporting nations as they are broadly similar to those given for Iran. Countries such as Libya, Saudi Arabia and the Gulf states are dependent on oil for virtually all their export earnings, so their general export price level will be almost identical to that cited for oil exports. This is not the case in Iran, however, which is also a major exporter of carpets and more recently has started exporting some manufactured goods, including cars, to neighbouring states. It is apparent that the price increases for Iran's non-petroleum exports, which also excludes natural gas piped abroad, have been much less impressive than those for oil exports. Nevertheless, even these non-oil exports have become more expensive in recent years, especially since 1974, as local wage levels and hence manufacturing costs have risen rapidly as a consequence of the oil boom. Fortunately, demand for non-oil exports such as Persian carpets appears to be relatively price inelastic, perhaps because they are usually regarded as luxury goods, and consequently the cost increases have had no adverse effect on production or employment within the country.

At first sight the prices obtained for the Turkish exports appear to have risen faster than those of Iran's non-oil exports. Appearances can be deceptive, however, because prices for both countries are denominated in the local currency, and while the Iranian rial has been appreciating in value, the Turkish lira has been depreciating as already mentioned in the previous chapter. In real terms Turkey has undoubtedly worsened its position much more than any of the other countries cited in the table as far as its purchasing power to acquire imports is concerned. Israel's currency has been depreciating even faster than Turkey's, so rapidly in fact that its export prices are quoted in U.S. dollars rather than Israeli pounds. Using this measure, Israel's position appears much better than that of Turkey, especially since 1972, as the price of citrus produce has risen rapidly owing to buoyant conditions in world markets. The economic recession in the West did not affect demand for items such as citrus produce, which forms a relatively insignificant part of consumer spending. In addition citrus produce are low-priced in comparison to many other food items, and may even have acquired the status of inferior goods which are used as substitutes for other more expensive goods when income levels fall.

All the other countries cited in Table 6.2 are dependent on cotton for a large portion of their export receipts, apart from Jordan, whose dependence on phosphates has already been discussed. The upward trend in prices for Egyptian and Sudanese long staple cotton has been much more marked in recent years than that for lower-grade Syrian cotton. To some extent this reflects the fact that Syria has more competitors, for there are few other countries producing high-grade cotton similar in quality to that of Egypt or the Sudan. Egyptian cotton[8] is of such high quality that it is exported, while at the same time the country actually imports lower-grade cotton for use in that part of the textile industry which produces cheap, but inferior, goods for the low-income market locally. Low-grade cotton from Syria is often blended with synthetic fibres for use in cheap clothing, while Egyptian cotton is seldom used in this way. Demand for high quality cotton goods may be less price elastic than that for lower-grade produce, because it is essentially from a quality conscious, high-income market. Unfortunately, Egypt has not been able to gain as much foreign exchange as might be expected from these favourable price trends, because a large portion of the country's cotton exports are sent to the Soviet Union to help pay off the heavy debt, incurred through the acquisition of military equipment, which has built up steadily during the last decade. Prospects for future cotton prices depend not only on world demand for staple items such as shirts and dresses, but also on how tastes change with respect to denim clothing. This kind of clothing has enjoyed widespread popularity for the last decade, but any switch to other substitutes as fashions change could undermine cotton prices and adversely affect export receipts of the major producers in the Middle East.

Although Syria has not fared as well as Egypt and Sudan in regard to its cotton prices, the price of its wool exports has been rising rapidly since 1972. A decade ago, man-made fibres threatened the position of wool in world markets, but in recent years wool has made a comeback, partly as a result of the success of the 'Woolmark' advertising campaign internationally. Wool is easier to tailor than synthetic substitutes, while at the same time research into fibres has lead to woollen worsted materials now having many of the advantages of man-made fibres as far as non-creasing is concerned in clothing. Prospects for wool exports therefore appear promising, and again the quality conscious high-income market in the West is not too concerned about the basic price of woollen fibres.[9] Syria's cereal exports have fared much worse than wool, as the price of barley has fluctuated erratically in world markets, declining in 1972, but then doubling, before deteriorating again. Given these violent price cycles,[10] and the growing local demand for cereals within Syria, it is not surprising that increasingly cereals are absorbed in the protected local market rather than exported. Jordan has had a similar experience with its exports from the Jordan valley, and the price of tomatoes, the main export commodity, was only slightly higher in 1974 in money terms than in 1971. This meant it was much lower in real terms as far as its contribution to Jordan's ability to purchase imported goods was concerned.

THE EXPANDING IMPORT MARKET

There will clearly be a close relationship between the change in the level of exports in any region and import changes, especially if value figures are used as in this study, taking account of the prices of traded commodities as well as quantities. Table 6.3, illustrating the growth of Middle East imports, shows how the major petroleum exporters are accounting for an increasing share of the region's import market, a trend that was accentuated by the remarkable oil price rises of 1974. Iran has of course long been the main import market in the Middle East, but the gap between Iran and Israel has steadily increased, even though Israel remains the second-largest market in the region, according to the latest published figures available at the time of writing.[11] It seems likely, however, that by 1975 Saudi Arabia in fact had overtaken Israel and become the second-largest importer in the Middle East, as a consequence of its vast oil revenues, although up-to-date import data is not available to confirm this. If this is the case it would be paradoxical that a largely desert state, with a small indigenous population still consisting of nomads for a large part, was able to import more than a country such as Turkey, which has a population at least five times as large, and a much more sophisticated economic structure. Yet import expenditure actually fell in 1975 in non-oil exporting states such as Turkey and Israel, and in real terms the drop was much greater than is indicated by the money values for imports cited in Table 6.3. Ironically, the drop in real import expenditure was accentuated by the negative income effect caused by the need for both countries to continue to purchase oil imports at the new inflated prices.

The increased petroleum revenues has not only widened the gap between the oil-exporting states and non-Arab Middle Eastern states such as Turkey and Israel as far as imports are concerned, but also caused a widening of the market differential between the Arab states themselves. Expenditure on imports rose only slowly in Egypt, Syria, the Sudan and Jordan between 1968 and 1973. In real terms the increase was in fact

TABLE 6.3. Growth of imports into the Middle East (values in millions of U.S. dollars)

Country	1968	1969	1970	1971	1972	1973	1974	1975
Iran	1384	1527	1662	1873	2409	3401	5672	7976
Israel	1093	1302	1422	1780	1955	2955	4179	4128
Turkey	770	754	894	1087	1508	2049	3720	3488
Saudi Arabia	563	747	692	806	1125	1974	3473	N/A
Libya	645	676	554	701	1043	1807	2762	N/A
Egypt	666	638	787	920	899	906	2348	2302
Iraq	404	440	509	694	713	906	2273	N/A
Kuwait	611	646	625	650	797	1051	1554	N/A
Lebanon	521	532	568	677	849	1333	N/A	N/A
Syria	303	368	357	438	545	613	1230	1182
Sudan	258	266	311	355	353	436	642	623
Jordan	161	190	184	215	267	331	488	455
North Yemen	N/A	36	32	37	80	123	190	204
South Yemen	203	218	201	158	149	171	187	N/A

Source: U.N., *Monthly Bulletin of Statistics*, April 1976.

negligible, as these countries, like many other Third World nations, experienced balance of payments difficulties throughout the period. In 1974, however, all these countries were able to spend a much larger amount on imports, owing to credits advanced by their fellow Arab oil-producing states, although a large portion of these credits were used in fact to finance petroleum imports. Jordan was the only country allowed to continue purchasing petroleum at pre-1974 prices, through the benevolence of Saudi Arabia; but this was halted by 1976, as some of the oil supplied at concessionary prices was being resold to third parties. In addition, by 1975, the oil-exporting nations were becoming less generous in extending credits to the poorer Arab states, as they appraised their own import needs and started thinking more about returns to themselves on the oil revenues being recycled. Imports therefore fell in 1975 in Egypt, Syria, Sudan and Jordan, as Table 6.3 shows, and in the future it seems these countries will increasingly have to import in line with their own capacity to pay, as the spirit of Arab solidarity which followed the October 1973 war gradually fades away and the oil pro-ducers put their own national self-interest first.[12]

In many ways the arbitrary distribution of oil wealth is unfortunate in the Arab world; Egypt, for example, has a much greater need for imports than Libya, but yet the latter has a larger capacity to import. Countries like Egypt and Syria which have achieved a measure of in-dustrialisation, find themselves experiencing foreign exchange bottle-necks which are a major obstacle to further development. At the same time, other states such as Saudi Arabia or Libya lack the trained per-sonnel and basic infrastructure easily to make use of foreign exchange earnings for local development. Ships carrying import consignments often have to wait at the ports of Saudi Arabia and the Gulf states for over 6 weeks before they can unload; and even when equipment is brought ashore there is in most cases a long delay before it is installed. A large proportion of funds are being spent indiscriminately on imports of expensive consumer durables such as luxury cars, while those non-oil states with manufacturing sectors cannot afford to replace existing machinery.[13] Consequently, their production suffers as did Egypt's textile industry in the 1960s, as well as the Helwan iron and steel plant. Clearly this is not the way to foster self-sustaining development within the Middle Eastern region as a whole. The import figures for South Yemen illustrate this vividly, as they show how one forgotten corner of the Arab world can fare badly, despite the boom conditions elsewhere. Its level of imports had to be cut back dramatically following the with-drawal of British troops in the 1960s and the subsequent loss in invisible earnings from their local spending. Since then its level of imports declined and, even in money terms, the 1974 value was well below that of 6 years earlier. Whether the reopening of the Suez Canal may help South Yemen's trade again, through increasing transit earnings, remains to be seen.

Only a few countries in the Middle East compile detailed records of their import prices.[14] The four countries cited in Table 6.4, however, all

TABLE 6.4. Import prices in selected Middle East economies

Country	1969	1970	1971	1972	1973	1974
Iran	96	100	102	111	125	143
Israel	98	100	102	109	142	193
Turkey	83	100	148	159	175	N/A
Sudan	96	100	107	116	N/A	N/A

Note: Base 1970 = 100.
Source: I.M.F., *International Financial Statistics*, April 1976.

appear to have suffered from rapid inflation in the cost of their imports, with Turkey faring the worst up until 1973. Prices in all the countries are admittedly denominated in terms of local currencies, which in the case of countries with depreciating currencies such as Turkey or Israel, makes the situation look especially bleak. A major portion of the rapid import price rise which Israelis experienced from 1973 onwards, can be attributed to the reduction in value of the Israeli pound following the setback in the October 1973 war. Nevertheless, neither Israel or Turkey have suffered a deterioration in their commodity terms of trade over the period, as the import price rises are less than the rise in export prices cited in Table 6.2. The prices for Israeli exports must be converted from dollars into the local currency before this result emerges, however. Israel has not suffered any deterioration in its income terms of trade either; foreign consumers have been prepared to pay higher prices for the country's citrus produce, which is relatively low-priced in any case, as already mentioned. Turkey in contrast has suffered, as its rising import prices have not resulted in any substantial cut in expenditure on goods from abroad, probably because many are necessary capital goods imports. At the same time the escalating price of exports has contributed to a substantial fall in demand for Turkish products abroad, since demand for them appears to be both more price and more income elastic than demand for Israeli produce.

In contrast to the Israeli pound and the Turkish lira, the Iranian rial has been steadily appreciating in value in recent years. Nevertheless, as Table 6.4 shows, even in Iran's case there has been a steady rise in the price of imports. Given the rapid rise in Iran's export prices in 1974, the country has, however, experienced a substantial improvement in its terms of trade position, and it is clearly much better placed than any of the non-oil-producing Middle Eastern countries to meet the escalating costs of imports from the industrialised world. In so far as these price increases in imported industrial goods are due to high wage settlements in the West brought about through trade union pressure, it can be argued that the countries of the Third World need a countervailing force to offset this. There is no doubt that in this imperfect market situation, the Organisation of Petroleum Exporting Countries, acting as a cartel, can serve as such a force to maintain the trading position of its members.[15] Sudan typifies more closely the situation prevailing in much of the Third World, because, although like Iran it is faced with rising import prices, it has not been in a position to exert pressure on its industrialised customers with respect to its export prices. Long staple cotton did fare well, it is true, in 1974, as already mentioned, but this boom may prove short-lived and, in the meanwhile, the relentless upward pressure on import prices will continue. During the 1969–74 period this has happened despite the fact that the Sudanese pound has maintained its value, unlike the currencies of most of the non-oil-exporters in the Middle East.

AID AND CAPITAL INFLOWS

A country's ability to import will of course be determined by its total foreign exchange receipts, comprising not only payments for visible exports, but also invisible earnings including aid and capital inflows. For the Middle East as a whole there has been a net private capital outflow in recent years. The investments made in the West by private companies and individuals from the oil-exporting nations greatly exceed the value of private investment coming into the region from outside. Given the vast amounts of capital generated through the oil industry in relation to the low absorptive capacity of the less populous producers, the large outward flow of investment funds is hardly surprising.[16] Private investors are after all concerned to get the highest possible returns on their funds, and these are unlikely to be great where complementary inputs are in short supply, such as labour, managerial expertise and basic infrastructure. In these circumstances the establishment of new industrial plants is likely to prove costly, especially where these complementary inputs have to be brought in from abroad. It may, in addition, take a long time before such investments become profitable, owing to the lack of experience of both the workforce and management. If these factors discourage local investors from keeping funds in their own countries, it is not likely that foreign investors will have much inducement to finance new projects. Normally Western investors look for situations where there are identifiable externalities; but these are often conspicuously lacking in the Middle East. For example, investment in a capital goods industry, or in intermediate production of components, is likely to be more profitable if the firms making the final products from these manufactured inputs are located in the same area. There are few cities in the Middle East apart from in Egypt and Iran where vertical linkages of this kind between different stages of production have been established.

Even where investment opportunities are available, and the existence of linkages is apparent, foreign investors have often been reluctant to commit themselves to new schemes on account of political uncertainty. The Arab–Israeli conflict, of course, has not helped in this respect, especially as far as potentially favourable areas for investment such as the Suez Canal Zone are concerned. Since the interim peace agreement between Egypt and Israel, prospects for investment in this front-line area have naturally improved.[17] Elsewhere, however, the situation remains uncertain, and few outside financiers would regard areas such as the West Bank of the Jordan, Gaza, or even Syria as safe areas for investment. Apart from the Arab–Israeli conflict, the continuing crisis in Lebanon between the religious communities has also undermined the confidence of foreign investors, especially as Beirut was hitherto considered the safest haven for private funds in the Middle East. Other conflicts in the region, such as Turkey's involvement in Cyprus and the internal agitation of the Kurds in Iraq, have had much less impact.

Of perhaps greater significance as a deterrent to foreign private investment is the left-wing political stance of many of the governments of the area. Private investors are unwilling to place their funds where there is any risk of nationalisation, especially if there are threats to seize assets without awarding adequate compensation. In Egypt, for example, most of the existing industry was nationalised in the early

1960s by Nasser, and compensation was awarded in the form of non-redeemable government bonds which yielded only low returns. Elsewhere, as in the case of the assets of the Western oil companies taken over recently in Saudi Arabia and the Gulf, compensation is awarded out of the future profits which the governments anticipate the installations will make under state ownership. In Iraq and Iran, where the Western oil companies' assets were taken over much earlier in order that these states could control their own production levels, compensation was even less generous.[18] When governments which favour free enterprise, such as that of Iran, adopt a hostile attitude to certain types of foreign capital, it is not surprising that investors take a much more jaundiced view of countries like Syria, Iraq, or South Yemen, where the governments profess a socialist ideology.

To some extent the tide of Arab socialism has started to ebb however, as Egypt's revision of economic policy under Sadat illustrates. There a new 'Open Door' policy has been adopted on foreign investment, which provides for 5-year tax holidays on new investment and free repatriation of profits. In addition, foreign firms establishing themselves in the free zones of the Suez Canal area can import any necessary inputs free of duty, as already mentioned in the previous chapter. Firms within the free zones are exempt from Egypt's profit-sharing law, whereby a quarter of the profits must be distributed to the workers. In addition, firms are also free from the law on worker participation in management which was enacted in 1961 under the Arab socialist measures. In effect this earlier legislation no longer applies in the free zones, and foreign investment is encouraged in all fields except real estate for non-industrial purposes. This last exemption was made in order to prevent land speculation of the type that is so prevalent elsewhere in the Middle East. The 'Open Door' policy is essentially designed to harness private investment for productive use, in order to augment employment opportunities within Egypt. To date most of the investment has been in tourism and banking rather than manufacturing industry, but it is perhaps too soon to judge the success of the policy.[19]

The Jordanian Government has always been in favour of a vigorous private sector in the economy, and consequently it has an investment encouragement law which gives generous incentives to foreign firms. A tax holiday of 6 years is allowed for new industries established in the Amman area, which extends to a 9-year exemption period in the provinces outside the capital. In 1975 company law was further liberalised to make it easier for foreign firms to set up local subsidiaries, without having to go through any complicated registration procedures similar to those elsewhere in the Arab world. In Jordan, as in other countries, encouragement is given to companies organised on a joint venture basis where the local partner holds at least half of the subscribed capital. Foreign investors often prefer to deal in this way in any case as it ensures their subsidiary can draw upon local expertise who are acquainted with domestic market conditions. In addition, if the local partner has some political influence, it may also be a safeguard against nationalisation, at least as long as the political status quo is maintained.

Compared with the size of private foreign investment in the Middle East, the amount of finance provided by foreign governments and international aid agencies has been enormous. Much of this assistance has, however, been to finance the purchase of foreign military equipment rather than to aid civilian projects. In so far as this is the case, this aid contributes little to economic development. When Israel purchases a Phantom jet, or Egypt a MiG fighter, the positive multiplier effects are felt in the United States or the Soviet Union and not in the Middle East.[20] Where external finance is used therefore merely for the purchase of defence equipment, it makes little contribution to self-sustaining economic growth, as military supplies are usually viewed as consumption items rather than investment goods.[21] Instead the country may get saddled with huge debts, as has happened in the case of Egypt. The final column of Table 6.5 shows that Egypt's debt service payments amount to almost one-third of its total export receipts. Israel is in a similar position, although Syria and Jordan have not been so adversely affected by the conflict as their debt figures indicate.

The problem of debt, of course, only arises when external financial assistance is in the form of loans rather than grants. Increasingly, assistance to the Third World is through lending, however, and as far as the Middle East is concerned, most finance takes this form. Usually there is a grant element in the loan, nevertheless, although this may be greater at the start of the repayment periods than later on. The problem with this kind of aid is that the debt burden gradually builds up, yet the less developed country in urgent need of financial assistance may be tempted to take the short-term view and neglect the future. Countries such as Algeria and Tunisia were offered substantial assistance by France, following their independence, on what appeared to be very generous terms, as there was a 5-year moratorium on payments. Once this period was finished, both countries found themselves in payments difficulties as a result of their debt. Fortunately, the oil price increases in 1974 eased Algeria's position,[22] and Tunisia's growing foreign exchange receipts from tourism have helped it to finance the repayments.

TABLE 6.5. Aid inflows to the Arab world in 1972 (millions U.S. $)

Recipient	Western sources	Allocation (%)	Communist sources	Allocation (%)	Total	Allocation (%)	Debt service payments as a proportion of export receipts (%)
Algeria	112	19	150	23	262	22	14
Egypt	35	6	170	26	205	17	31
Somalia	24	4	110*	17	134	11	3
Tunisia	114	20	—	—	114	9	16
Iraq	10	2	100	15	110	9	2
Jordan	103	18	—	—	103	9	7
Morocco	91	16	5	1	96	8	8
Sudan	37	6	14	2	51	4	12
Syria	10	2	41	6	51	4	10
Mauritania	22	4	20*	3	42	3	8
North Yemen	15	3	22	3	37	3	N/A
South Yemen	5	1	16*	3	21	2	N/A

Note: * 1971.
Source: Kuwait Fund for Arab Economic Development, *The Arab World: Key Indicators*, Tables 7.1–7.5.

The Sudan, which got itself into a similar state of indebtedness, however, as the table indicates, is in a less fortunate position. Despite a rise in earnings from cotton exports, its debt service payments have become even worse since 1972, in relation to the value of its export receipts.

In the Middle East, as in other parts of the Third World, there is little relationship between the amounts of foreign aid provided and the financial needs of the recipient country. The motivation for aid is primarily political, and the distribution of disbursements illustrated in Table 6.5 reflects this fact. Algeria was the largest single recipient of recorded foreign assistance in 1972, despite the country's significance as a petroleum exporter. In addition, Algeria obtained large amounts of foreign exchange earnings through remittances sent back by its workers resident in France. Nevertheless, although France ran a substantial trade deficit with Algeria, owing to its demand for oil imports, it still provided aid in return for a continuing stake in the country's petroleum industry. Egypt, the second-largest aid recipient, was in greater need of assistance, but most of its aid came from Communist sources, and was tied to the purchase of equipment from eastern Europe. As one of the major policy objectives of Egypt's planners was to increase industrial employment, these funds were borrowed to finance industrial expansion. East European aid has mostly taken the form, however, of providing heavy capital equipment for industries such as iron and steel, or highly sophisticated machinery for the textile industry. Industries installing such equipment are by nature capital intensive, and little additional employment is provided. In the case of the textile industry the employment effect may in fact be negative, and the result is technologically induced unemployment or, in practice in Egypt, industrial underemployment.[23] It should be noted that the recorded figure for Communist aid to Egypt does not include military aid, details of which are still not available, despite the publicity over Egypt's indebtedness through defence purchases.

At first sight it may seem strange that Somalia should be the third-largest recipient of aid in the Arab world, despite the fact that it has only 3 million people. The Soviet Union has, however, made substantial sums available as aid, in return for the use of naval facilities at Somalia's ports. There is little doubt that the Soviet Union is more concerned with the country's strategic importance as an Indian Ocean base, at the gateway to the Red Sea, than with the fate of the 3 million indigenous inhabitants. Iraq and Syria also receive substantial aid from the Soviet Union, for largely political reasons as it ensures a Soviet voice is heard in these two professedly socialist states which play a major role in Arab politics. Syria is, of course, in much greater need of aid than Iraq, which is a substantial oil exporter, yet it is perhaps ironic that it is the latter which receives a much greater share. A similar situation prevails, however, with respect to Western aid to Tunisia and Jordan; the needs of King Hussein's country are much greater, given that over half the population of the East Bank are Palestinian refugees, many of whom still live in camps. The amounts of money provided for the United Nations Relief and Welfare Agency, the main body dealing with the refugees, are pitifully small in relation to the amounts of bilateral aid committed to prestige projects elsewhere in the Arab world which benefit few people.[24] In the same manner, Table 6.5 shows that it is those Arab countries which are poorest, the Sudan, and North and South Yemen, which receive least aid in relation to the size of their populations and their foreign exchange needs. What is clearly required is a change in the pattern of aid disbursements if aid is to be used to foster development. In the case of the West, however, there is no doubt its aid could easily be increased, as its commitments are well below those of the Eastern bloc, which has much fewer resources at its disposal.

Under the present world monetary system, members of the International Monetary Fund are allocated quotas of financial reserves, including Special Drawing Rights, on the basis of their subscriptions to the Fund. These subscriptions are in turn related to the size of each member's gross national product and its share in world trade. In practice this results in the rich industrialised nations getting the major share of global reserves, while the poor nations of the Third World are allocated minimal amounts, despite their chronic shortages of foreign exchange in many cases.[25] This pattern of allocation is reflected in the regional distribution of holdings of Special Drawing Rights within the Middle East, as Table 6.6 shows. Oil-rich Kuwait has alone received a majority of the total Rights allocated to the region, while Iran has also obtained a substantial share. In contrast the poorer countries of the Middle East such as Egypt and the Sudan, which experience great balance of payments difficulties, have been allocated only very small amounts of Special Drawing Rights. Of course, to an extent, this distribution of rights reflects the willingness of countries to hold their reserves in this form, rather than in some other type of internationally accepted form of asset such as gold or convertible currencies. Nevertheless, it is unfortunate that it is those countries that have the greatest need to import essential foodstuffs and capital goods for development projects, that at the same time lack the means to pay for such items. Special Drawing Rights allocations can be regarded as a form of aid in that they serve to

TABLE 6.6. Allocation of Special Drawing Rights to Fund members in the Middle East (millions U.S.$)

Country	1970	1971	1972	1973	1974	1975	Average allocation	Proportion of regional allocation
Kuwait	21	22	22	24	313	671	179	57
Iran	1	1	37	45	55	65	34	11
Turkey	—	5	42	34	42	32	26	8
Iraq	—	13	25	24	28	27	20	6
Egypt	—	8	6	38	38	17	18	6
Israel	—	14	32	34	3	2	14	4
Sudan	—	—	5	16	26	9	9	3
Jordan	3	6	8	9	9	9	7	2
South Yemen	2	5	8	9	4	4	5	2

Source: I.M.F., *International Financial Statistics*, March 1976.

increase a country's capacity to import; since, unlike bilateral aid, these funds are not tied, they are in many respects of much greater value. As with other forms of aid, however, in so far as the countries under review are concerned, their allocation has done little to help development. Critics of the existing international monetary system need look no further than the Middle East to see how it results in opportunities being wasted.

RECYCLING OF SURPLUS REVENUES

Since the oil price bonanza of 1974, there has been a considerable amount written in the financial press in the West on the subject of oil revenue recycling.[26] Given the limited capacity of many of the leading oil producers to absorb a high amount of imports from the industrialised world, the governments of many of the oil-consuming nations were concerned that they would be in a state of permanent balance of payments deficit.. To a large extent, in retrospect, these fears have proved to be ill-founded, initially because the demand for oil from the major consuming nations turned out to be less inelastic with respect to price than was first suspected. The volume of oil consumption did fall as a result of the higher prices, and this price effect was compounded in 1975 by a negative income effect due to the recession in the industrialised world. In the longer term it seems likely that the income elasticity of demand for oil may have fallen permanently; existing energy substitutes are being used, and the quest for alternative resources is speeding up. Some long-term benefit may therefore accrue from the oil price increases, if in fact they do lead to an increase in world energy supplies and to consumers becoming more conservation-minded. At the time of writing it seems that some of the large consuming nations such as Germany and Japan are managing to reflate their economies successfully without running into payments deficit again on account of oil imports.

The economies of the West have also been helped by the fact that the capacity of the oil-exporting nations to absorb their imports has proved greater than expected.[27] Iran's balance of payments surplus in 1975 was only half the level predicted, and it is expected that by 1980 only the less populous countries, such as Saudi Arabia and Kuwait, will continue running substantial surpluses. Table 6.7 gives some indication of the relative magnitudes of the financial surpluses generated in the Middle East, as these are closely linked to the size of a country's reserves. The enormous increase in the reserve assets of the major petroleum exporting countries in 1974 is shown—a consequence of the oil price increases.

TABLE 6.7. Growth of Middle East financial reserves

Country	International reserves 1975 (million U.S.$)	Growth of reserves: 1969 = 100						
		1969	1970	1971	1972	1973	1974	1975
Saudi Arabia	23,319	100	109	238	412	639	2353	3842
Iran	8697	100	67	200	310	399	2704	2805
Iraq	2727	100	121	164	221	502	1151	948
Libya	2195	100	173	290	319	232	394	239
Lebanon	1674*	100	111	157	194	248	482	—
Kuwait	1655	100	112	158	199	275	768	909
Israel	1183	100	110	184	313	462	314	310
Turkey	1064	100	176	311	572	865	760	434
Syria	835*	100	93	149	229	815	141	—
Jordan	486	100	97	96	102	119	133	185
Egypt	356*	100	115	103	96	250	245	—
Qatar	71	100	112	135	180	475	450	—
South Yemen	67*	100	106	115	120	136	121	—
Sudan	36	100	60	77	98	168	341	100

Note: * Data for 1974.
Source: I.M.F., *International Financial Statistics*, March 1976.

Saudi Arabia's reserves are the largest in the world, while Iran's are comparable in size to those of the major industrial nations of western Europe.[28] The increase in reserves in Kuwait and the less populous Gulf states has also been dramatic, but it is interesting to note that, by 1975, there was actually a contraction in reserves in both Libya and Iraq. Libya in fact did not experience any large increase in financial reserves after 1970, partly because of the country's high propensity to import, but also because of the cutbacks in production. Initially these were due to the dispute between the Libyan Government and the oil companies; but more recently there has been a deliberate policy of conservation. A further drain on Libya's reserves has been the revolutionary regime's willingness to lend financial support to Third World countries and revolutionary movements.

Compared to the reserves of the oil exporters, those of the non-oil-exporting economies of the Middle East are very small, as Table 6.7 indicates. Saudi Arabia's reserve levels are an astonishing 65 times greater than those of Egypt, while Libya's are over six times as large. Yet, as already mentioned, Egypt's capacity to absorb imports is much greater and the country's development is being stunted by foreign exchange bottlenecks. Meanwhile, reserve levels have fallen slightly in Egypt as a consequence of the October 1973 war, although the fall was not as large as in other front-line states. Syria's reserves fell to below a fifth of their former level, while Israel's dropped by almost one-third, and this decline continued into 1975. Jordan was in a more favourable position, partly because the government decided not to open a front on its own territory, nor to become too involved on the Syrian front. Confidence in the Jordanian economy was therefore maintained, and the authorities did not have to use their reserves to support the dinar. At the same time the rising price for phosphates, Jordan's main export, during the 1974–75 period helped to strengthen the economy. Lebanon was not involved in the conflict either, and its reserve position improved as increased oil revenues started coming into the Beirut banking system from the Gulf. Unfortunately this favourable situation was brought to a sudden halt by the country's own civil war.[29] It is paradoxical, but hardly surprising, that the poorest countries in the region, South Yemen and Sudan—those in greatest need of imports for development purposes—are also the countries with the lowest reserves. Saudi Arabia's reserves are 650 times larger than the Sudan's. The Sudanese have barely enough reserves to serve for intervention purposes to support their currency, and there is little available to finance any balance of payments deficit. The authorities therefore have to curtail even essential imports, and recently the situation has deteriorated still further as reserve levels fell by almost 350 per cent between 1974 and 1975. This means that Sudan's reserve assets in 1975 were at the same level as 6 years earlier while, over the same period, Saudi Arabia's reserves have increased over 38-fold.

As the more populous states in the Middle East all have a high propensity to import, recycling will only remain a long-term issue in countries such as Saudi Arabia or the Gulf states. In these countries the oil revenue boom has created a real dilemma concerning the best means of securing future income in a situation of great uncertainty.[30] Given the low current income requirements, these nations have the choice of either conserving their valuable oil assets as an insurance for tomorrow, or else acquiring assets abroad which promise a favourable rate of return. To some extent these oil producers, including Libya, as already mentioned, have opted for conservation. At the same time, however, countries like Saudi Arabia are reluctant to introduce any long-term embargo on oil exports to the West, despite the action following the 1973 war when supplies to the Netherlands and the United States were temporarily suspended. This is because the Saudis recognise their interdependence with the West. Although the industrialised countries need their oil, at the same time the Riyadh government wants manufactured imports and defence equipment. Any collapse of the Western economy would spell ruin for Saudi Arabia. Hence the reluctance to cut back too far in production.[31] For the same reason the Saudis have let their opposition be known to any proposals for large oil price increases similar to those of 1974, as they do not want to force a further recession on the West. Instead they would like to see oil prices rising slowly in line with the oil consumers' ability to pay as their economies are gradually reflated again.

If oil production is to continue at levels beyond the capacity of the less populous countries to absorb the revenues generated, this necessitates them holding some form of internationally acceptable assets. In the past the safest form of asset was undoubtedly gold; it was not only prized as a metal, but was also acceptable as a medium of exchange for international monetary purposes. Although there was no interest earned on gold, unlike on currency assets, it nevertheless was regarded by many as a better store of value, as it was less likely to depreciate than national currencies. In the late 1960s therefore, many Middle Eastern states held a major portion of their reserve assets in the form of gold as Table 6.8 shows. The monetary authorities in Lebanon acted very conservatively and held over four-fifths of the country's reserves in gold, as it was

TABLE 6.8. Official gold holdings in the Middle East

Country	Amount (million U.S.$)							Proportion of reserve assets as gold						
	1969	1970	1971	1972	1973	1974	1975	1969	1970	1971	1972	1973	1974	1975
Lebanon	287	287	350	350	389	395	—	83	75	64	52	45	24	—
Iraq	193	143	156	156	173	176	168	40	31	26	20	11	5	6
Kuwait	86	86	94	94	120	150	163	47	42	33	26	24	11	10
Iran	158	131	142	142	158	160	153	51	63	23	15	13	2	2
Turkey	117	127	130	136	151	153	146	48	29	17	10	7	8	14
Saudi Arabia	119	119	117	117	130	132	126	20	18	8	5	3	1	1
Egypt	93	93	92	92	103	104	—	64	56	62	66	28	29	—
Libya	85	85	93	93	103	104	100	9	5	3	3	5	3	5
Israel	46	43	47	43	46	47	45	11	10	6	4	3	4	4
Syria	28	28	30	30	33	34	—	47	51	34	22	7	4	—
Jordan	30	28	30	30	34	34	33	11	11	12	11	11	10	7
Qatar	6	6	7	7	8	8	—	41	37	33	24	10	11	—

Source: I.M.F., *International Financial Statistics*, March 1976.

believed this would encourage outsiders to maintain confidence in the Beirut banking system. Countries such as Iraq, Kuwait and Saudi Arabia held gold partly because they lacked financial expertise at that time and were distrustful of paper assets. To some extent this lack of trust was justified, for Kuwait lost heavily on its sterling assets when the United Kingdom devalued in 1967, and again lost after floating in 1971. The prime motivation of countries such as Egypt and Syria in holding gold was security: they feared that if they held a major portion of their assets in Western securities, this might make them vulnerable in time of war as their reserves would run the risk of being frozen. The last, but certainly not the least, important reason for holding gold was the fact that the metal had been valued for its own sake for centuries throughout most of the Middle East. It is not surprising that countries such as Qatar held substantial amounts in relation to their total reserves, because it was an important centre for gold smuggling in the past.[32] The figures cited in Table 6.8, however, only refer to official reserves of gold held by the central banks or monetary agencies of the countries concerned. Private holdings of gold, of course, probably greatly exceed these official reserves, especially in Iran, Iraq and the Gulf.

With the enormous growth in reserves in the Middle East during the last 5 years, there has been a steady decline in the proportion of gold held, especially in the major oil-exporting nations. To a large extent this reflects the fact that there is simply not enough gold available in the world. If countries such as Saudi Arabia held all their assets in gold, it would absorb all the world's total stocks. The oil surplus countries of the Middle East had therefore little choice but to hold other types of internationally acceptable assets, such as convertible currencies or Special Drawing Rights. They have been encouraged to do this by the demonitisation of gold, which has resulted in the metal losing some of its mystique.[33] In addition, the interest now paid on Special Drawing Rights has prompted some of the major oil producers to open deposits with the International Monetary Fund under the so-called 'oil facility' agreement, whereby the money can be used by oil-consuming nations running deficits. Saudi Arabia deposited the equivalent of 2250 millions of S.D.R.s under the agreement, Iran 990 millions and Kuwait 685 millions. Of the smaller oil-exporting nations, the Union of Arab Emirates subscribed 100 million S.D.R.s and Oman one-fifth of this amount. Together the Middle Eastern countries have thus deposited over four-fifths of the total amount agreed under the 'oil facility' arrangements, the other major subscribers being Venezuela and Nigeria.

These arrangements have provided a major vehicle for oil revenue recycling and have proved attractive to both producing and consuming nations. From the point of view of the producing nations, S.D.R.s are undoubtedly more attractive than most national currencies because of their stability. Swiss francs and Deutschmarks are, admittedly, even more attractive as a form of deposit, owing to the possibility of making a capital gain with appreciation. Deposits in Swiss francs, however, have earned a negative rate of interest since 1974—that is the customer pays the bank for the privilege of holding an account denominated in the local currency, rather than the reverse which is the usual banking practice. British Government Treasury Bills earn much higher interest rates than S.D.R.s, but these are insufficient to compensate any oil-producing nations holding such assets for the decline in the value of sterling. In these circumstances the future role of S.D.R.s as a store of value as well as a medium of exchange seems assured.[34] At the same time the Western countries welcomed the 'oil facility' arrangements because it enabled them to run larger deficits than they otherwise could have done, which meant the deflationary impact of the oil price rises on their domestic production and employment was much less than it might have been in the absence of the agreement.

In relation to the amounts of assets held in the form of foreign government securities or Special Drawing Rights, the funds placed in stock markets in the West by private Middle East investors is limited. The depressed state of Western stock markets in 1974–75 was partly responsible for this, although ironically it was largely brought about by the economic recession following the oil price increases. In addition the uncertainty prevailing in the stock markets over share prices was a deterrent to those Middle East investors who lacked financial expertise in any case; government securities, with a guaranteed return, even on a low level, appeared a safer bet. Kuwaiti investors, more accustomed to dealing in these markets, are much more venturesome than Saudi Arabians. In any case, there are more people concerned with foreign investments in the Gulf States because the oil revenue spreads down to a large number of people. In Saudi Arabia the government itself made the majority of the decisions about assets because it held most of the revenue itself and did not implement redistribution measures. There was no scheme in Saudi Arabia similar to Kuwait's land purchase programme, whereby the government bought small plots of land at grossly inflated prices as a means of redistributing income to property-owning citizens. These private beneficiaries have placed funds in a multitude of Western companies, whereas the Saudi authorities prefer to deal on a simple government to government basis and to hold state securities.

The opposition expressed from many quarters concerning the investment of Middle Eastern funds in leading companies in the West has undoubtedly had an inhibiting effect on private capital flows.[35] When the Iranian Government acquired a substantial share of the equity of Krupps, the Ruhr-based heavy engineering and armaments firm, the take-over was opposed by many in Germany.[36] Similarly there was widespread opposition from United States politicians and the financial community to the Saudi acquisition of a major shareholding in two medium-sized banking institutions. It is paradoxical however, that there should be such opposition when for years Western companies held all the most valuable assets that the Middle East had to offer. The Middle Eastern involvement in the financial markets of the West is insignificant in comparison to the historical involvement the other way.

Often Middle East investors prefer to place funds in property rather than industrial equities. This is a further reason for opposition in the West to these investments. The critics argue that it only aggravates the problem of speculation in land, office accommodation, and apartment complexes. Within the Middle East itself there is a growing amount of speculation in property, which is not surprising in countries where landowners are a powerful economic force and land is regarded as the most important means of production. Investors see land as a safer form of asset than industrial stock, and the promise of substantial capital gains is usually self-fulfilling in a situation of widespread speculation. As most Middle East.funds placed abroad privately have gone into city centre developments in the major capitals of the West where prices are already high, opposition must be expected. In so far as recycled oil revenues are invested in property, this results in a redistribution of income in the West away from industry. Thus, in other words, nonproductive activities gain, while those economic activities which make the major contribution to development and trade lose, which means in the long run there will be a negative effect on world economic growth.

The Middle East is therefore closely integrated with the international economy, not only with respect to trade, but also because of outward and inward capital movements. Today these external linkages are undoubtedly stronger than ever, despite the import substitution policies adopted by the countries of the Middle East. As the region's economy has grown, its impact on the international economy has been positive as far as income is concerned, although historically the region itself has not benefited as much from trade as it might have had there been different prices prevailing for traded commodities. To some extent the radical Egyptian economist, Samir Amin, is correct when he asserts,

'Outward orientated development is not development, but development of underdevelopment'.[37] In addition, as far as the benefit to the international economy of Middle East trade is concerned, the positive income effect must be set against the negative distributional effects associated with recycling. These are undoubtedly aggravated by the high propensity of the Middle East to spend on defence equipment, essentially a non-productive consumer good which contributes little to investment. When aid and loans are used for this purpose, there is an opportunity cost not so much from the point of view of the region, but in the country acting as donor or lender. It is the industrialised countries that after all have to divert more resources into production for military purposes, while at the same time the funds being made available as loans or aid could be used instead to finance their own domestic investment. A lasting peace in the Middle East, and consequent curtailment in defence spending, would benefit not only the region itself, but the world economy at large.

Notes

CHAPTER 1

1. For a detailed account of Egypt's emergence as a cotton exporter see Robert Owen, *Cotton and the Egyptian Economy 1820–1914* (Oxford University Press, 1969).
2. Estimated on the basis of figures from OPEC *Annual Statistical Bulletin* (1975).
3. An introductory outline of the vent for a surplus theory is given by Ronald Findlay, *Trade and Specialization* (Penguin, 1970), Chapter 4.
4. Yet much of Egyptian industry is capital intensive. See Robert Mabro, 'Industrial Growth, Agricultural Underemployment and the Lewis Model —The Egyptian Case 1937–1965', *Journal of Development Studies*, Vol. 3, No. 4 (1977) 322–51.
5. Only a limited number of copies are available in English. For details of the plan see Howard Bowen-Jones, 'Boom and Bottlenecks', *Financial Times Survey of Saudi Arabia*, 12 January 1976. For its trade implications see the article by the present author in the same supplement.
6. As is evident from the figures for manufacturing production issued by the Planning Ministries in both countries. A brief review of Iraq's mediocre development record is given by Keith McLachlan and Narsi Ghorban, *Oil Production, Revenues, and Economic Development*, Economist Intelligence Unit Special Report No. 18 (1974).
7. Further information on fertility trends is provided by Paul Schultz, 'Fertility Patterns and their Determinants in the Arab Middle East', in Charles Cooper and Sidney Alexander, *Economic Development and Population Growth in the Middle East* (Rand Corporation, 1971).
8. Robert Mabro, 'Employment and Wages in Dual Agriculture', *Oxford Economic Papers*, Vol. 23, No. 3 (1971) 401–17.
9. International Labour Organisation, *Rural Employment Problems in the U.A.R.* (Geneva, 1969).
10. Bent Hansen, 'Employment and Wages in Rural Egypt', *American Economic Review*, Vol. LIX (1969) 298–313.
11. In spite of this high population growth, per capita incomes have risen however in most countries in the area. See Galal Amin, *The Modernization of Poverty* (E. J. Brill, Leiden, 1974), Chapter 1.

12. In fact there is perhaps over-urbanisation. See Galal Amin, *The Modernization of Poverty*, (E. J. Brill, Leiden, 1974), Chapter 3.
13. Keith McLachlan, *Planning and Industrialisation in Iran* (Focus Research, 1975). See also earlier 1974 report on Iran by Focus Research.
14. Rodney Wilson 'Business Climate Remains Favourable for Foreign Investors and Contractors', *The Times Supplement on Egypt*, 26 March 1975. Also later article by the author in *The Times*, 5 November 1975.
15. Robert Stevens, *The Arabs' New Frontier: A History of the Kuwait Fund* (Temple Smith, London, 1973).
16. Robert Z. Aliber, 'Oil and the Money Crunch', *National Westminster Bank Review*, February 1975; Jan Tumlir, 'Oil Payments and Oil Debt in the World Economy', *Lloyds Bank Review* (June 1974).
17. Minos Zombanakis, 'Arab Funds and the Markets', *The Banker* (July 1974).
18. International Monetary Fund, *International Financial Statistics* (December 1975).
19. Although they will have to improve on their previous industrial performance as outlined by Julian Bharier, *Economic Development in Iran 1900–1970* (Oxford University Press, 1971).
20. See the Focus Research Report on Iraq (London, 1975).
21. As the authors of most introductory texts on development emphasise at the start. See Walter Elkan, *An Introduction to Development Economics* (Penguin, 1973). Also Matthew McQueen, *The Economics of Development* (Weidenfeld and Nicolson, 1973).
22. A useful background book on Libya has been written by Ruth First, *Libya: The Elusive Revolution* (Penguin, 1974).

CHAPTER 2

1. For a summary of these developments see M. Clauson, H. Landsberg and L. Alexander, *The Agricultural Potential of the Middle East* (Rand Corporation, New York, 1972).
2. G. Baer, *A History of Landownership in Modern Egypt 1800–1950* (Oxford University Press, 1962).
3. Doreen Warriner, *Land Reform and Development in the Middle East, a Study of Egypt, Syria and Iraq* (Oxford University Press, 1957).
4. See Gabriel Saab, *The Egyptian Agrarian Reform 1952–1962* (Oxford University Press, 1967).
5. See Food and Agricultural Organisation of the United Nations, *Country Reports of Iraq and Syria to World Land Reform Conference* (Rome, 1966), Mimeographed.
6. R. M. Ghonemy, 'Economic and Institutional Organizations of Egyptian

Agriculture since 1952', in P. J. Vatikiotis (ed.) *Egypt Since the Revolution,* (Allen and Unwin, London, 1968).

7. Ann Lambton, *The Persian Land Reform 1962–66* (Oxford University Press, 1969).

8. A useful discussion of some of the general economic issues involved is given by K. L. Bachman and Christensen, 'The Economics of Farm Size' in H. M. Southworth and B. F. Johnston (eds.), *Agricultural Development and Economic Growth* (Cornell University Press, New York, 1967). These issues are discussed in a Middle East context by Doreen Warriner, 'Relation between Land Reform and Development', National Bank of Cairo 50th Anniversary Commemoration Lectures (Cairo, 1955). Reprinted in C. Eicher and L. Witt (eds.), *Agriculture in Economic Development* (McGraw-Hill, New York, 1964).

9. E. Eshag and A. M. Kamal, 'Agrarian Reform in the United Arab Republic (Egypt)', *Bulletin of the Oxford Institute of Economics and Statistics,* Vol. 30 (May 1968), pp. 96–8.

10. Doreen Warriner, *Land Reform in Principle and Practice* (Oxford University Press, 1969), Chapters 1 and 4.

11. K. S. McLachlan, 'Land Reform in Iran', in W. B. Fisher (ed.), *The Cambridge History of Iran* (Cambridge University Press, 1968), Vol. 1, p. 684ff.

12. This was the case in Egypt, for example—See Mahmoud Abdel-Fadil, *Development, Income Distribution and Social Change in Rural Egypt 1952–1970,* University of Cambridge, Department of Applied Economics Research Monograph (March 1975), Chapter 5.

13. Doreen Warriner 'Employment and Income Aspects of Recent Agrarian Reforms in the Middle East', *International Labour Review,* Vol. 101, (1970). See also R. M. Ghonemy 'Land Reform and Economic Development in the Middle East', *Land Economics,* Vol. 44, (1968).

14. For an account of recent changes in Turkey see Oddvar Aresvik, *The Agricultural Development of Turkey* (Praeger, New York, 1975), Chapters 2, 3 and 4 especially. The last deals with agricultural services.

15. See Food and Agricultural Organization of the United Nations, *Country Report of Egypt to.World Land Reform Conference* (Rome, 1966), Mimeographed.

16. Ann Lambton, 'Land Reform and the Rural Cooperative Societies', in Ehsan Yar Shaler (ed.), *Iran Faces the Seventies* (Praeger, New York, 1971), Chapter 1.

17. See reports of Syria and Iraq to the *1966 World Land Reform Conference* (see Note 5).

18. J. D. Atkinson, *Handbook of Egyptian Irrigation* (Cairo, 1934).

19. Mohamed Youssef El Sarki, *La Monoculture du Coton en Egypte et le Developpement Economique,* (Librairie Droz, Geneva, 1964).

20. C. Warren 'The High Aswan Dam and New Trends in Egyptian Agriculture', *Foreign Agriculture,* Vol. 7, (1969).

21 Rodney Wilson, 'Egypt', *The Times Supplement on the Arab Renaissance*, 20 March 1975, p. 6.

22. Egypt historically tended to opt for the former. See Galal A. Amin, *Food Supply and Economic Development with Special Reference to Egypt* (Cass, London, 1966).

23. Of course, technical innovations can help, but these are usually costly to implement. An interesting case study of the applicability of one type of innovation has been undertaken by J. J. Fried and M. C. Edlund, *Desalting Technology for Middle Eastern Agriculture: An Economic Case* (Praeger, New York, 1971), Chapters 3–7 especially.

24. The United States Public Law 480 food aid programme, although well intentioned, resulted in depressed food prices in the recipient countries of the Middle East.

25. Data from Food and Agriculture Organisation of the United Nations, *Production Yearbook* (Rome, 1975).

26. For a classic account of this 'Revolution' see Lester R. Brown, *Seeds of Change: The Green Revolution and Development in the 1970s* (Praeger, New York, 1970).

27. Harry Myint, *South East Asia's Economy*, (Penguin, London, 1971). Chapter 2 discusses the Green Revolution.

28. One useful study was conducted by R. M. Stern, 'The Price-Responsiveness of Egyptian Cotton Producers', *Kyklos*, Vol. 12, (1959).

29. Which can ultimately result in forced procurement, as in the Soviet Union in the 1920s and 1930s.

30. This was stressed at the *CENTO Conference on National and Regional Livestock Development Policy* (CENTO, Tehran, 1970). See especially the country situation papers, p. 26ff.

31. B. Hansen and M. El Tomy, 'The Seasonal Employment Profile on Egyptian Agriculture', *Journal of Development Studies* (1965), No. 1.

32. A large proportion of citrus fruit exports have been included in the bilateral trade deals with the Soviet Union, and given Egypt's state of indebtedness, it has little choice but to continue exporting under these rather one-sided agreements. Some vegetable exports have been reaching the West in recent years.

33. A classic exposition of the problem in the Middle East was given by Gunnar Myrdal, 'Development and Underdevelopment' National Bank of Egypt Fiftieth Anniversary Commemoration Lectures (Cairo, 1956), pp. 9–10 and 47–51. Reprinted in Gerald M. Meier, *Leading Issues in Economic Development* (Oxford University Press, 1964), pp. 479–84.

34. Rodney Wilson, 'Fruiterer to the Arab World', *The Times Supplement on Beirut*, 27 June 1975, p. 3.

35. Especially in neighbouring Saudi Arabia.

36. *The Arab World: Key Indicators*, The Kuwait Fund for Arab Economic Development (Kuwait, April 1975), Table 6.4, p. 40.

CHAPTER 3

1. For detailed information on how this was achieved see Fuad Rouhani, *A History of O.P.E.C.* (Praeger, 1971), Chapters 1–4, 15 and 16 especially.
2. A critical account of Saudi Arabia's economic progress is given by Fred Halliday, *Arabia Without Sultans* (Penguin, 1974), Chapter 2.
3. Z. Y. Hershlag, *Economic Structure of the Middle East* (E. J. Brill, Leiden, 1975). Chapter 3 is on the economic interpretation of Arab socialism.
4. Jahangir Amuzegar and M. Ali Fekrat, *Iran: Economic Development Under Dualistic Conditions* (University of Chicago Press, 1971), Chapter 2.
5. The latest book on Egypt is by Robert Mabro, *The Egyptian Economy* (Oxford University Press, 1974). Chapter 8 deals with structural changes in the economy.
6. Susan Paine, *Exporting Workers: The Turkish Case*, Cambridge, Department of Applied Economics Occasional Paper 41 (1974). Krane, R. E. (ed.), *Manpower Mobility Across Cultural Boundaries: Social, Economic and Legal Aspects. The Case of Turkey*, Vol. 16, in Social, Economic and Political Studies of the Middle East (E. J. Brill, Leiden, 1975).
7. Israel's development performance is assessed by D. Horowitz, *The Enigma of Economic Growth: A Case Study of Israel* (Praeger, New York, 1972).
8. Three useful introductory texts on the economies of these countries are:
   (1) H. S. Odeh, *Economic Development of Jordan 1954–71* (Jordanian Press Foundation, Amman, 1973).
   (2) G. A. Salem, *Modernization Without Revolution: Lebanon's Experience* (E. J. Brill, Leiden, 1974).
   (3) S. Al-Akhrass, *Revolutionary Change and Modernization in the Arab World: The Case of Syria* (Atlas, Damascus, 1972).
9. See Rodney Wilson, *Industrialization and Foreign Capital*, (Focus Research Report on Egypt, London, 1974).
10. State-owned companies have played a key role in this industrialisation in Turkey. See G. Schachter and B. Gohen, 'The Efficiency of State Economic Enterprises in Forging Development in Turkey', *Annals of Public and Co-operative Economy*, Vol. 44(2), (1973), pp. 165–79.
11. A recent evaluation of Saudi Arabia's development record has been made by S. H. Hitti and G. T. Abed, 'Economy and Finances of Saudi Arabia', *I.M.F. Staff Papers*, 21(2) (1974). See also R. Knaverhase, 'Saudi Arabia's Economy at the Beginning of the 1970s', *Middle East Journal*, 28(2) (1974).
12. Despite its harsh desert conditions, Libya does offer scope for import substitution of agricultural commodites. See J. A. Allan (ed.), *Libya: Agriculture and Economic Development* (Cass, London, 1973).
13. Funds were invested in import substitutes even in the first decade of this century. See Samir Radwan, *Capital Formation in Egyptian Industry and Agriculture 1887–1967* (Ithaca Press, London, 1974), Chapters 3 and 5 especially.

14. Two comprehensive accounts of the first post-revolutionary decade are provided by:
  (1) Bent Hansen and G. Marzouk, *Development and Economic Policy in the U.A.R. (Egypt)* (North Holland Publishing, Amsterdam, 1965), Chapters 5 and 6.
  (2) Donald Mead, *Growth and Structural Change in the Egyptian Economy* (Yale University Press, 1967), Chapter 5 especially.
15. Hassan El Saaty and Gordon K. Hibabayashi, *Industrialization in Alexandria*, American University at Cairo, 1959. K. M. Barbour, *The Growth, Location and Structure of Egyptian Industry* (Praeger, New York, 1972).
16. P. K. O'Brien, *The Revolution in Egypt's Economic System* (Oxford University Press, 1966).
17. *Middle East Economic Digest*, Vol. 18, No. 8, 22 February 1974, p.199ff.
18. *Egyptian Gazette*, 18 March and 31 March 1974. *Middle East Economic Digest*, Vol. 18, No. 22, 31 May, 1974, p. 623.
19. Rodney Wilson, *The Times Supplement on the Arab Renaissance*, 20 March 1975.
20. Which meant relatively high wages for those lucky enough to find industrial employment in the urban areas. See Mahmoud Abdel-Fadil, *Development, Income Distribution and Social Change in Rural Egypt 1952-1970* (Cambridge University Press, 1975).
21. The size of the labour absorption problem in Egypt can be seen from the study by Mostafa Nagi, *Labour Force and Employment in Egypt* (Praeger, New York, 1971), Chapters 1 and 6 especially.
22. For a brief survey of some of the issues involved in the adoption of intermediate technology see E. F. Schumacher, *Small is Beautiful* (Abacus, 1974). A more thorough account is provided by Amartya Sen, *Employment, Technology and Development* (Clarendon Press, Oxford, 1975).
23. The most comprehensive work on Iran's development is by Julian Bharier, *Economic Development in Iran* (Oxford University Press, 1971).
24. Walter Elkan, *Iran's Human Resources* (Focus Research, London, 1974).
25. For an account of industrialisation trends see R. G. Looney, *The Economic Development of Iran 1959-1981* (Praeger Special Studies, New York, 1974).
26. Diversification in these fields is discussed by J. P. C. Carey and A. G. Carey, 'Industrial Growth and Development Planning in Iran', *Middle East Journal*, Vol. 29 (1975), pp. 1-15.
27. Though Iran historically has boasted a high level of skill. See Charles Issawi, *The Economic History of Iran 1800-1919* (Centre for Middle Eastern Studies, University of Chicago, 1971).
28. H. B. Chenery, 'Patterns of Industrial Growth', *American Economic Review*, September 1960, pp. 624-54.
29. Mohamed Yamin, *Import Substitution and the Growth of Manufacturing Industry in Iran 1955-72*, M.A. Thesis, University of Durham, June 1975.
30. Linkages between the petroleum sector and the rest of the economy are

considered by A. Melamid, 'Petroleum Product Distribution and the Evolution of Economic Regions in Iran', *Geographic Review*, Vol. 65 (1975), pp. 510–25.

31. The company publishes its own journal giving details of its operations, *Iran Oil Journal*. The summer and autumn issues of 1975 give details of some of the company's diversification plans.

CHAPTER 4

1. Details of import controls are presented in the International Monetary Fund *Annual Reports on Exchange Restrictions*, published in Washington each year.
2. For a general review of the issues involved see Bela Balassa, *The Structure of Protection in Developing Countries* (Johns Hopkins Press, Baltimore, 1971).
3. Julian Bharier, *Economic Development in Iran 1900–1970* (Oxford University Press, 1970) Chapter 6.
4. Bahrain was the main centre for this trade.
5. Most of the pioneering work on effective protection was carried out by W. M. Corden. See his article on 'The Structure of a Tariff System and the Effective Protective Rate', *Journal of Political Economy*, Vol. 74 (1966), pp. 221–37. Reprinted in Jagdish Bhagiwati (ed.), *International Trade*, (Penguin, 1969), Chapter 12.
6. A detailed analysis of the Iranian data was undertaken by Mohamed Yamin, *Import Substitution in Iran*, M.A. Thesis, University of Durham, 1975.
7. This formula was developed by W. M. Corden (see Note 5).
8. Details of Saudi tariff levels are given in a *Business Directory of Saudi Arabia*, published by the Business Aids Division of University Securities Limited (London, 1974), pp. 48–9.
9. Rodney Wilson, 'Big Importer', *The Financial Times Survey of Saudi Arabia*, 12 January 1976, p. 20.
10. The measures were introduced in late 1974, once the oil revenue boom started making its impact felt locally.
11. Rodney Wilson, *Industrialization and Foreign Capital* (Focus Research Report on Egypt, London, 1974), pp. 15–22.
12. Rodney Wilson, 'Revival of Canal Traffic is Key to Success', *The Times Supplement on Cairo*, 7 October 1976, p. 27.
13. A brief summary of recent economic developments in Oman is given by Ann Fyfe, 'Copper: the Next Potential Money Spinner', *The Times Supplement on Oman*, 15 November 1975, p. 4.
14. See the I.M.F., *Annual Report on Exchange Restrictions* (Washington, 1975), p. 219ff.
15. Ibid., p. 142.

16. Rodney Wilson, 'Caught in a Trap over Soviet Debt', *The Times Supplement on Egypt*, 5 November 1975, p. 5.
17. Given Israel's high rate of inflation in recent years, this means importers face considerable loss on these deposits in real, if not in money, terms.
18. For a description of how bilateral arrangements work see P. T. Ellsworth and J. Clark Leith, *The International Economy* (Collier Macmillan, London, 1975), p. 380ff.
19. An introductory explanation of these mechanisms is given by Leland B. Yeager, *International Monetary Relations* (Harper and Row, New York, 1966), Chapter 2. For a more detailed study of the operation of exchange markets see Paul Einzig, *A Textbook of Foreign Exchange* (Macmillan, London, 1966).
20. I.M.F., *Annual Report on Exchange Restrictions* (Washington, 1975), p. 220.
21. Before 1972 when tourists were allowed to convert officially at the parallel market rate, there was a substantial black market in currency which the authorities found impossible to eradicate.
22. Peter Field, 'O.P.E.C. Leads the Search for Stable World Currency', *Middle East Economic Digest*, 27 June 1975, p. 9. 'Wrangling and Sparring Protracted', *The Arab Economist*, July 1975, p. 54ff. Also 'Severing Links with the Dollar, The Shape of Things to Come', *The Arab Economist*, May 1975, p. 18ff.
23. H. A. Merklein, 'How Energy Relates to World Monetary Problems', *The Arab Economist*, June 1975, p. 42ff.
24. Ann Crossfield, 'Importing Inflation', *The Financial Times Survey of the United Arab Emirates*, 22 May 1975, p. 21.
25. H. A. Merklein (see Note 23).
26. In so far as the policy was successful, and the currency was overhauled, it also made imports more competitive in the local market. This must have had a detrimental effect on local industry.
27. Little outside funding has become available at the time of writing.
28. Especially given Jordan's ambitious development objectives. See Rodney Wilson, 'Rapid Growth is Daunting Target', *The Times Supplement on Jordan*, 25 May 1975, p. 2.

CHAPTER 5

1. The case for regional economic integration in the Middle East is similar to that for other areas of the Third World. For an appraisal of the general issues involved see R. F. Mikesell, 'The Theory of Common Markets and Developing Countries', in Peter Robson (ed.), *International Economic Integration* (Penguin, 1971), Chapter 9.
2. This point was stressed by David Garrick, 'Regional Integration and Economic Development in the Middle East', *Middle East Affairs*, Vol. XII, No. 9 (1961) 294–300.

3. Problems of economic integration in the Gulf are dealt with by Saad Andari, *Kuwait: Developing a Mini Economy*, M.A. Thesis, University of Durham, 1975.
4. Details of the operation of the Middle East Supply Centre are presented by E. M. H. Lloyd, *Food and Inflation in the Middle East 1940–45* (Stanford University Press, 1956). There is also a standard work on the subject by M. W. Wilmington, *The Middle East Supply Centre* (State University of New York Press, 1972).
5. When both countries became one United Arab Republic from 1958–1961. For a discussion of the wider political and economic issues involved in the union see Robert Stephens, *Nasser*, (Pelican, 1971).
6. The most comprehensive account of the operation of the Arab Common Market is given by Albert Musrey, *An Arab Common Market* (Praeger, New York, 1969).
7. For a critical account of the operation of the market, see Z. Y. Hershlag, *Economic Structure of the Middle East* (E. J. Brill, Leiden, 1975), Chapter 12.
8. The original agreement is available in English: 'Document relating to Decision No. 17 of the Arab Economic Unity Council: The Arab Common Market.'
9. See Rouhollah Ramazani, *The Middle East and the European Common Market* (University Press of Virginia, 1964), Chapters 6 and 7 especially.
10. See Galal Amin, *The Modernization of Poverty* (E. J. Brill, Leiden, 1974) p. 28ff.
11. This was also the problem with respect to the more limited economic union proposed for North Africa. See Abderrahman Roban, *The Prospects for an Economic Community in North Africa*, Praeger, 1973, Chapters 3 and 7. Similarly, prospects for increased trade between Turkey, Iran and Pakistan did not appear promising. See Bill Hale and Julian Bharier, *CENTO, R.C.D. and the Northern Tier: A Political and Economic Appraisal*, Middle Eastern Studies, Vol. 7, Part 3 (1972).
12. The Israeli Statistical Abstract provides information on immigration into the country: Table II_2, II_3, etc. in the abstract for each year.
13. Estimates of the total number of Palestinian exiles are compiled by UNRWA (United National Relief and Welfare Agency), as well as the Israeli Central Bureau of Statistics. Unfortunately, but not surprisingly, the figures conflict.
14. English translation of the Agreement, Chapter 1.
15. For a brief account of recent trends in education in the Arab world, and the productiveness of investment in education, see Galal Amin, *The Modernization of Poverty* (E. J. Brill, Leiden, 1974), p. 61ff.
16. An introduction to the literature and a bibliography is given by G. M. Meier, *Leading Issues in Economic Development* (Oxford University Press, 1971), p. 313ff.

17. See Shimeon Amir, *Israel's Development Co-operation with Africa, Asia and Latin America* (Praeger, New York, 1974).
18. An interesting study of the West Bank economy has recently been published. Vivian Bull, *The West Bank—Is It Viable?* (Lexington, Massachusetts, 1975).
19. See, for example, H. W. Richardson, *Elements of Regional Economics* (Penguin, 1969).
20. Kamal Sayegh, *Oil and Arab Regional Development* (Praeger, 1968), Chapter 7.
21. Rodney Wilson, 'Caught in Trap over Soviet Debt', *The Times Supplement on Egypt*, 5 November 1975.
22. For details of aid to the Arab world, both from within the region and outside, see *The Arab World: Key Indicators*, Kuwait Fund for Arab Economic Development (K.F.A.E.D.), April 1976, Tables 7.1-7.4.
23. The most comprehensive account of the Fund's operations is provided by Robert Stephens, *The Arabs New Frontier: A History of the Kuwait Fund* (Temple Smith, London, 1973).
24. An introduction to techniques of project appraisal is given in G. M. Meier, *Leading Issues in Development Economics* (Oxford University Press, 1970), p. 340ff.
25. Up-to-date figures on the Fund's lending are provided in its own *Annual Reports* published in Kuwait.
26. Information on the operation of these organizations is given in their *Annual Reports*, published in English. A more detailed account of both bodies is given by Tony Underwood, *Inter-Arab Financial Flows*, M.A. Thesis, University of Durham, 1974.
27. This body was sponsored by the Kuwait Fund. See Z. A. Nasr, *The Kuwait Fund Scheme for the Guarantee of Inter Arab Investments* (K.F.A.E.D., May 1972). Also, Abdlatif Y. Al-Hamad, *Building up Development Orientated Institutions in Arab Countries* (K.F.A.E.D., October 1972).
28. A point even the Director of the Kuwait Fund admits. See A. Y. Al-Hamad, *Investing Surplus Oil Revenues* (K.F.A.E.D., April 1974). See also the Director's address to the European Institute of Business Administration, *Arab Funds and International Economic Cooperation* (K.F.A.E.D., November 1973).
29. See Bill Hale and Julian Bharier, *CENTO, R.C.D. and the Northern Tier*, Middle Eastern Studies, Vol. 7, Part 3 (1972).

CHAPTER 6

1. Especially capital goods.
2. For an analysis of the implications of this, see Keith McLachlan and Nasir Ghorban, *Oil Production, Revenues and Economic Development:*

Prospects for Iran, Iraq, Saudi Arabia, Kuwait, U.A.E., Oman, Qatar and Bahrain, Economist Intelligence Unit Report 18, London, 1974. Iraq, p. 28ff; Kuwait, p. 42ff.

3. The largest fruit packing factory in Israel and the occupied territories is located in Gaza.
4. Rodney Wilson, 'Rapid Growth is Daunting Target', *The Times Supplement on Jordan,* 25 May 1976, p. 2.
5. The export sector in both economies was largely an enclave one, although in Egypt there were strong linkages between cotton and domestic economic activities.
6. This will undoubtedly increase if Saudi Arabia's ambitious development plan for 1975–80 is implemented, since this envisages that an additional 500,000 migrants will be required.
7. In fact, apart from the 1973–74 period, the oil-exporting countries present a classic example of the Prebisch thesis.
8. Long staple cotton.
9. Trends in all these basic commodity prices are given in the FAO *Annual Production Yearbooks,* published in Rome.
10. Which cause a 'cobweb' effect through the demand and supply interactions.
11. For earlier details of relative trade positions, see J. D. Coppock, *Foreign Trade of the Middle East* (A.U.B., Beirut, 1966). Also Lee E. Preston, *Trade Patterns in the Middle East* (American Enterprise Institute for Public Policy Research, Washington, 1970).
12. Though that is not to say that OPEC solidarity will be reduced; the gains from a cartel arrangement are obvious to all parties.
13. The emergence of these imbalances is described by Galal Amin, *The Modernization of Poverty* (E. J. Brill, Leiden, 1974), Chapter 1.
14. Figures for the other states only cover local retail prices of a limited range of imported commodities.
15. The most up-to-date account of OPEC operations is given by Mana Saeed Al-Otaiba, *O.P.E.C. and the Petroleum Industry* (Croom Helm, London, 1975), Part 2 especially.
16. Michael Field, *One Hundred Million Dollars a Day* (Sidgwick and Jackson, London, 1975).
17. Signed in September, 1975.
18. For details of Iran's early negotiations with the companies see Jahangir Amuzegar and Mohamed Ali Fekrat, *Iran: Economic Development under Dualistic Conditions* (University of Chicago Press, 1972), Chapter 3.
19. Rodney Wilson, *Industrialization and Foreign Capital* (Focus Research Report on Egypt, London, 1974), p. 15ff.
20. Z. Y. Hershlag, *Economic Structure of the Middle East* (E. J. Brill, Leiden, 1975), Chapter 11 deals with defence expenditure.
21. Unless it results in the establishment of a local armaments industry. See

L. Lockwood, 'Israel's Expanding Arms Industry', *Journal of Palestine Studies*, Vol. 1, No. 4 (1972) 73–91.

22. In addition, remittances from Algerians in France help. See M. Guillon, 'Les Repatriés d'Algèrie dans la Région Parisienne' *Annales de Géographie*, Vol. 83 (1974), pp. 644–75.

23. See Chapter 3 on import substitution—the Egyptian case.

24. And this is spread over Lebanon, Syria and Israel, as well as Jordan.

25. There have been several proposals to link S.D.R.s with aid. See Lord Kahn, 'SDRs and Aid', *Lloyds Bank Review*, No. 10, (October 1973), p. 1; also the reply by P. T. Bauer in the subsequent issue of the review, p. 42.

26. As well as in financial journals. See, for example, Robert Z. Aliber, 'Oil and the Money Crunch', *National Westminster Bank Review* (February 1975). Jan Tumlir, 'Oil Payments and Oil Debt in the World Economy', *Lloyds Bank Review* (June, 1974).

27. Gerald A. Pollack, 'Are the Oil Payments Deficits Manageable', *Princeton Essays in International Finance*, No. 111, International Finance Section, Princeton University, (June 1975).

28. For a useful background study of Saudi Arabia which throws light on its capacity to import, see Ramon Knauerhase, *The Saudi Arabian Economy* (Praeger, New York, 1975).

29. As a result of which severe exchange controls were introduced in 1975 and 1976.

30. Rodney Wilson, *Enigmas of a Rentier Economy: The Case of Saudi Arabia*, Centre for Middle East and Islamic Studies, Economic Research Paper No. 9 (1975), p. 12ff.

31. This interdependence is stressed by Abdlatif Y. Al-Hamad, *International Finance: An Arab Point of View* (paper published by Kuwait Fund for Arab Economic Development, October 1974).

32. Smuggling between the Gulf, India and Pakistan still continues on a large scale.

33. Robert Triffin, 'The Case for Demonetization of Gold', *Lloyds Bank Review* (January 1974), p. 1ff.

34. As well as a unit of account, now that leading Middle Eastern currencies are quoted in S.D.R.s.

35. For an Arab point of view see Abdlatif Y. Al-Hamad, *Arab Capital and International Finance* (Kuwait Fund for Arab Economic Development, November 1973).

36. Especially as the Shah has already made Iran the main military power in the Middle East.

37. Though his concern since leaving Egypt has been West Africa rather than the Middle East. See Samir Amin, *Neo Colonialism in West Africa* (Penguin, London, 1973), Introduction, p. XIVff.

Index